In-Fisherman
LIBRARY SERIES . . .

FRESHWATER
RIGS & RIGGINGS

Cutting Edge Presentation Paraphernalia

In-Fisherman LIBRARY SERIES . . .

FRESHWATER RIGS & RIGGINGS

Cutting Edge Presentation Paraphernalia

Expert Advice from North America's
Foremost Authority on Freshwater Fishing

THE IN-FISHERMAN STAFF

In-Fisherman

In-Fisherman Library Series . . .
The Complete Book of . . .

Freshwater Rigs & Riggings

Publisher *Mike Carney*
Associate Publisher *Steve Hoffman*
Editor In Chief *Doug Stange*
Editors *Dave Csanda, Steve Quinn, Matt Straw, Jeff Simpson*
Book Compiled by *Cory Schmidt*
Publisher Emeritus *Stu Legaard*
Copy Editor *Joann Phipps*
Layout & Design *Amy Jackson*
Editorial Assistant *Claudette Kitzman*
Cover *Brian Lindberg*

Freshwater Rigs & Riggings

First Edition

Library of Congress Cataloging-in-Publication Data
ISBN: 1-892947-49-8

Dedication

To every angler who, in striving to become a better angler, discovers along the way an abiding love for the process and practice of fishing and fish conservation.

Contents

Introduction

From the Editors—
A Word about This Book

In-Fisherman is famous for teaching anglers how to catch fish by employing the formula Fish + Location + Presentation = Success. Simply put, once an angler knows enough about a fish species to be able to locate the fish, the final step is making a lure or bait presentation tempting enough to fool the fish into biting. This requires a proper combination of rod, reel, and line, but also the right lure or bait choice fished on just the right rig or rigging.

Here, our staff takes a comprehensive look at the types of rigs and rigging that have been featured by In-Fisherman over the past 30 years. These rigs are as good as they get, the result of an elimination process that has taken place in the field with editors tinkering here and there, modifying and remodeling, until the rigs are just right for the various missions at hand.

Many rigs not only have multiple purposes, but can also be applied to multiple fish species. Quick-strike rigging, for example, has been used by staff members to catch pike, muskies, catfish, bass, stripers, walleyes, and more, with only a slight modification to the actual construction of the basic rig. Like most rigs, it's simple to understand and use—economical to make, too, once the components have been gathered.

Time and again, what we find is that the best anglers, like the best athletes, are better at the fundamentals of their sport because they're a lot more in tune with the details that affect performance. We offer you a chance to take a step beyond the rest of the crowd, here, using the finest rigs, discovered in several lifetimes' worth of exploratory fishing.

Key to Primary Species

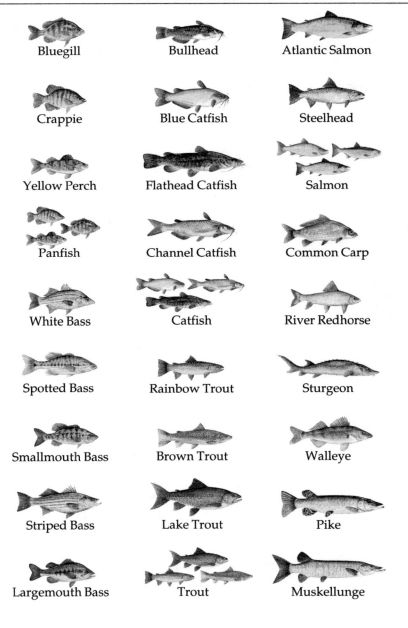

Bluegill

Bullhead

Atlantic Salmon

Crappie

Blue Catfish

Steelhead

Yellow Perch

Flathead Catfish

Salmon

Panfish

Channel Catfish

Common Carp

White Bass

Catfish

River Redhorse

Spotted Bass

Rainbow Trout

Sturgeon

Smallmouth Bass

Brown Trout

Walleye

Striped Bass

Lake Trout

Pike

Largemouth Bass

Trout

Muskellunge

Chapter 1

Bottom Rigs

Freeline & Fixed Sinker Rigs

THE MOST NATURAL APPROACH TO PRESENTATION

Unencumbered by weight, a freeline rig remains one of the most subtle and natural methods of presenting live-bait. All fish can be taken on this simple rig, but freelining is probably most widely used by largemouth bass anglers targeting trophy-class fish.

On many famous Florida bass waters—Okeechobee and Kissimmee lakes, and the St. Johns River—anglers freeline wild golden shiners near heavy cover to produce big largemouths. In now-storied California lakes—Clear, Miramar, and Castaic—bass hunters often freeline live crayfish for fish over 15 pounds. A freeline rig allows lively baitfish, frogs, crayfish, and other baits to behave as naturally as possible.

PRIMARY SPECIES

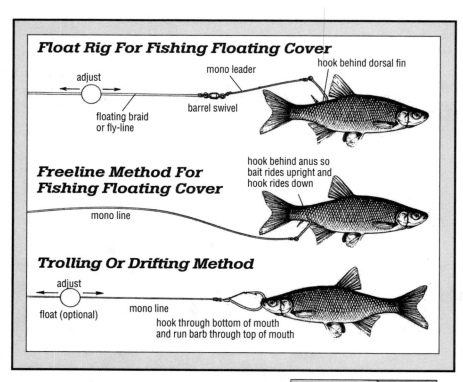

Float Rig For Fishing Floating Cover

adjust

mono leader

hook behind dorsal fin

barrel swivel

floating braid
or fly-line

Freeline Method For Fishing Floating Cover

mono line

hook behind anus so
bait rides upright and
hook rides down

Trolling Or Drifting Method

adjust

float (optional)

mono line

hook through bottom of mouth
and run barb through top of mouth

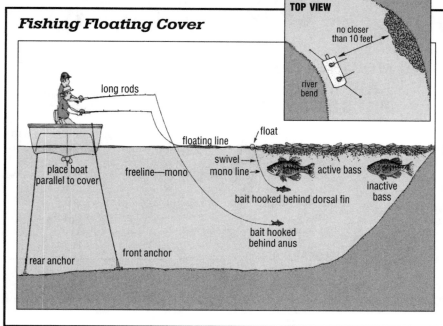

Fishing Floating Cover

TOP VIEW

no closer
than 10 feet

river
bend

long rods

floating line

float

place boat
parallel to cover

freeline—mono

swivel →
mono line →

active bass

inactive
bass

bait hooked behind dorsal fin

bait hooked
behind anus

rear anchor

front anchor

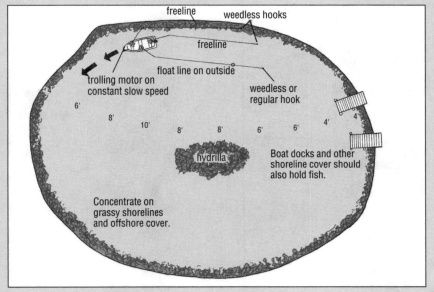

Trolling Or Drifting Multiple Rods In A Shallow Natural Lake

freeline

weedless hooks

freeline

float line on outside

trolling motor on constant slow speed

weedless or regular hook

4'

6'

8'

10'

8'

8'

6'

6'

4'

4'

hydrilla

Boat docks and other shoreline cover should also hold fish.

Concentrate on grassy shorelines and offshore cover.

1. Cruise lake to determine the 8-foot contour line.
2. Run two freelines and one float line for starters, covering the 8-foot zone.
3. Adjust according to strikes.

TACKLE

Rod & Reel—Choose a rod that allows for soft lob casts—7 to 12 feet and longer with a slow to moderate action, light to heavy power, and a soft tip. A spinning or casting reel with a smooth drag is suitable for most freeline applications.

Line—4- to 8-pound clear, green, or brown monofilament to match water color; fluorocarbon line for exceptionally clear water. Use heavier lines in heavy cover, and for larger baits and larger fish.

Sinker—None; freelining refers to fishing without weight.

Connections—None are necessary in most cases. If line twist becomes a problem, add a barrel swivel 1 to 3 feet above the hook.

Leader—In clear water or for wary fish, use a light monofilament or fluoro-carbon leader.

Knots—A strong, reliable line-to-hook connection, such as the Trilene knot. A snell knot is best for hooks with down-turned or up-turned eyes.

Hooks—Hook size and style depend on bait selection and cover conditions. For freelining large baitfish or frogs near weeds and other cover, try a #1 to 2/0 weed-less hook. In most other situations, use a light-wire octopus or wide-gap hook.

Natural Baits—Regardless of species, livebait must be healthy and vigorous. Best of all is bait captured from the water you're fishing. Wild, indigenous bait live in the environment, which means they react naturally when a predator approaches. Few fish can resist such an offering.

Livebait Rigging

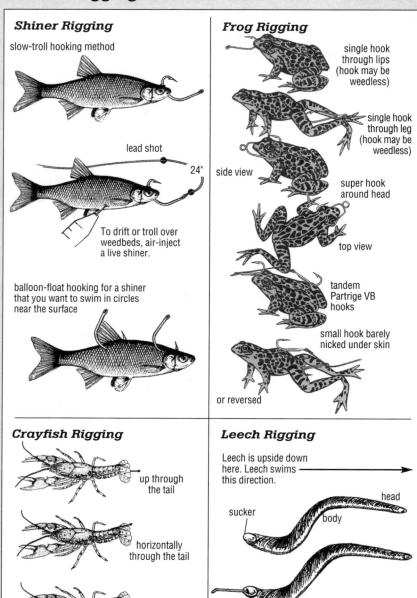

Shiner Rigging

slow-troll hooking method

lead shot

24"

To drift or troll over weedbeds, air-inject a live shiner.

balloon-float hooking for a shiner that you want to swim in circles near the surface

Frog Rigging

single hook through lips (hook may be weedless)

single hook through leg (hook may be weedless)

side view

super hook around head

top view

tandem Partrige VB hooks

small hook barely nicked under skin

or reversed

Crayfish Rigging

up through the tail

horizontally through the tail

horizontally through the crown

Leech Rigging

Leech is upside down here. Leech swims this direction.

head

sucker

body

standard hook placement

Common baits for bass include golden shiners, crayfish, leopard frogs, and waterdogs; smallmouth bass are particularly fond of ribbon leeches on a plain hook. Muskie and pike fishermen prefer large suckers, while channel catfish anglers sometimes freeline pieces of cutbait.

Tail-Clipping Minnows

Clip top off tail and the bait swims up; clip bottom and it swims down.

RIGGING WRINKLES

When you need to suspend a bait above a snaggy bottom or just keep it up near the surface, add a floating jighead or small in-line float. Clip the bottom portion of a minnow's tail fin and the minnow swims downward; clip the top of the fin and it swims up.

FISHING THE FREELINE RIG

Where & When—Fishing in shallow water and heavy cover, particularly thick vegetation, makes other presentations difficult. A freeline rig, though, can be dabbled above potential snags. Consider this simple hook-and-bait rig when targeting a large fish, a selective fish, or working a small area. Freelining wild bait also works when trying to call fish near the surface over shallow to mid-depth flats.

The freeline rig is especially effective when you allow the livebait to execute the presentation on its own, that is, working in place without rod action. Or slowly drift or troll a freelined bait. Trolling along weedlines, near the edges of brush and timber or other structures, is particularly effective.

Presentation—When fishing livebaits, particularly minnows, avoid pitching the bait off the hook or damaging it by casting too hard. Instead, use a slow, fluid sidearm swing, releasing line so the bait softly floats just above the water as it sails toward the target. Try not to lob the bait too far, so it contacts the water with excessive force. Avoid continual casting unless you're working a specific spot where you're sure a big fish is holding.

Pay attention to the signals your livebait sends up the line. Wild shiners, for example, often become nervous when a predator approaches, which you'll feel as light tap-tap-taps on the line or rod tip. When the tap-taps become a solid thump that usually means a fish has engulfed the bait. Once the fish has the bait completely in its mouth, reel slowly to retrieve slack line, then sweep the hook home.

SPLIT-SHOT RIGGING

The split-shot rig—a hook and a pinch-on sinker—can be tied in less than a minute. Break one off and it's no big deal. But don't let the simplicity of the rig fool you. Just because it's easy to tie and not particularly fancy to look at doesn't mean the rig's only for kids and panfish. True, the split-shot rig might be the best-producing sunfish rig of all time, but when fished properly it also accounts for larger fish.

Split-Shot Rigging

split shot pinched on line

6 inches to 3 feet

bait with small worm, reaper, or grub

TACKLE

Rod & Reel—A 6- to 8-foot slow- to moderate-action, medium-light-power spinning rod and a spinning reel with a longcast spool.

Line—4- to 8-pound-test monofilament.

Sinker—One to three pinch-on lead shot for basic rigging. The size and quantity of shot is determined by depth, current, and the size and type of bait. Shot placement determines bait action, especially with livebait. The closer the sinker lies to the bait, the less freely the bait can swim. Too far away, however, and you lose control of the bait, resulting in missed bites and more snags. Most often, attach the sinker 6 to18 inches from the hook.

Connections—None necessary in most cases. If line twist becomes a problem, add a barrel swivel several feet above the hook.

Leader—In clear water or in the presence of wary fish, use a light monofilament or fluorocarbon leader.

Knots—Connect hook to line with a Trilene knot.

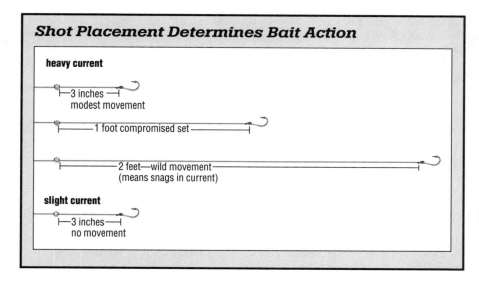

Shot Placement Determines Bait Action

heavy current

⊢—3 inches —⊣
modest movement

⊢—1 foot compromised set ————⊣

⊢————2 feet—wild movement————————⊣
(means snags in current)

slight current

⊢—3 inches —⊣
no movement

Hooks—Choose a #8 to #2 octopus-style hook for small leeches and minnows. For nightcrawlers, baitholder hooks with barbs on the shank work well for keeping bait secured on the hook. When using 3- to 6-inch soft-plastic baits for largemouth and spotted bass, tie on a #2 to 3/0 lightwire offset worm hook.

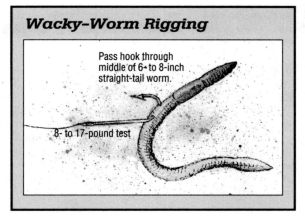

Natural Baits—The split-shot rig is popular with panfish anglers when small nightcrawlers, angleworms, and insect larva are baits of choice. The simplicity of the rig, however, lends itself to the use of almost any natural bait. Live golden shiners for bass, ribbon leeches for walleyes, cutbait for channel catfish, even crayfish and amphibians work well on a split-shot rig.

Soft Plastics—Plastic baits are often used on a split-shot rig as a finesse presentation for largemouth bass. Subtle 3- to 6-inch straight-tail worms, grubs, and lizards are productive options.

RIGGING WRINKLES

Due to the simplicity of this rig—changing something as basic as the sinker—makes it no longer a split-shot rig, though it still performs the same function. For instance, striped bass and catfish anglers often use a Rubbercor or Pinch-Grip sinker above a hook for a vertical presentation to suspended fish. Essentially,

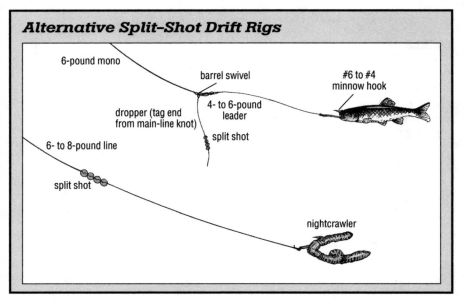

it's the same rig but employs a different sinker style to perform a different function. Anglers also use split-shot rigs to drift natural baits in rivers for steelhead and catfish.

FISHING THE SPLIT-SHOT RIG

Where & When—Due to the light weight of this rig, it's best in water shallower than 20 feet, and often shallower than 8 feet. While the rig is prone to snags, especially in rock, it's fairly trouble-free over clean sand or gravel bottoms. The split-shot rig also works well when dabbled vertically above bottom.

Presentation—The split-shot rig can be fished in many different ways. Cast it short distances and slowly retrieve it, or fish it stationary on the bottom. This rig also works when drifted downstream in light to moderate current in smaller rivers. Follow the drift with your rod tip to keep the bait bouncing naturally along the bottom.

SET RIGGING

Widely used by shore anglers, the set rig performs well for catfish, bullheads, stream trout, carp, and other fish that feed near shore over clean bottom areas. The set rig is often called a dropper-loop rig for the looped snells fastened to the main line above the sinker. Typically, one to three pretied snells are tied 12 to 18 inches above the sinker for presenting multiple baits simultaneously, state laws allowing.

PRIMARY SPECIES

TACKLE

Rod & Reel—A 6- to 7-foot moderate-action, medium-power spinning or casting rod; a medium-capacity spinning or baitcasting reel.

Line—6- to 12-pound-test monofilament.

Sinker—Bell sinkers from 1/2 to 2 ounces work best. Tie a single weight to the end of the line to anchor the rig in place.

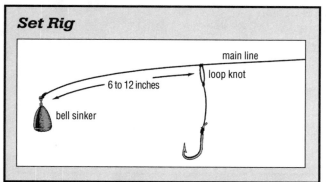

Set Rig

main line

loop knot

6 to 12 inches

bell sinker

Connections—None.

Leader—Pretied 6- to 12-inch snells are available from most hook companies. Tie as many of these short snells to your main line as are legal—one or two droppers is most common.

Knots—To secure pretied snells to the main line use an improved clinch knot, leaving a long tag end to attach the sinker with another clinch knot. To tie your own snells, use a snell knot to fasten the hook to the leader. At the end of the snell, tie a double surgeon's loop to provide a connection point.

Hooks—Hook choice depends largely on the bait, cover conditions, and the size of the fish you're targeting. Baitholder-style hooks are a popular choice. Most pretied snells have a #6 to #1 baitholder hook with a barbed shank. The barbs on these hooks work especially well when rigging nightcrawlers. For presenting salmon eggs, marshmallows, or other soft nugget-shaped baits for trout, a #10 to #6 egg or octopus-style hook works best. Since some soft baits don't hold well on single hooks, a #14 to #6 treble hook might be necessary. When fishing pliable dough baits for catfish or carp, special trebles with a small spring on the shank grip these baits well. When using chicken entrails or congealed blood that doesn't stay attached to single hooks, #6 to #1 treble hooks are a better choice. For presenting live baitfish or leeches, use #8 to #2 octopus hooks.

Natural Baits—The set rig is often used to present nightcrawlers or angleworms. Live leeches, small minnows, cutbait, and frogs also are common bait options for set rigs.

Prepared Baits—Many companies offer dough baits that can be shaped onto a hook for trout and catfish. These baits are infused with flavors and colors. Scouting the prepared bait section of the tackle shop yields flavors such as cheese, garlic, shad, blood, and even barbecue. Other commercial bait options include fish eggs, marshmallows, lunch meat, and canned sweet corn. These baits work best for stocked trout and carp.

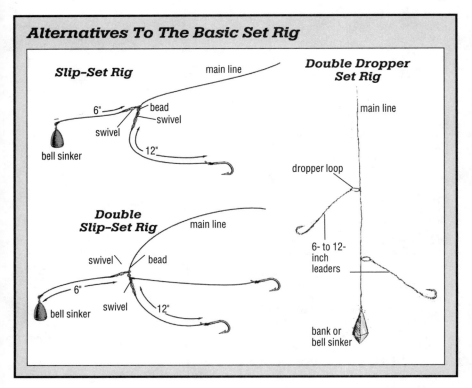

Alternatives To The Basic Set Rig

Slip-Set Rig
main line
6"
bead
swivel
swivel
bell sinker
12"

Double Dropper Set Rig
main line
dropper loop
6- to 12-inch leaders
bank or bell sinker

Double Slip-Set Rig
main line
swivel
bead
6"
swivel
12"
bell sinker

RIGGING WRINKLES

Productive variations of this rig, particularly the swivel-set slip rig, include the addition of swivels and plastic beads, which transform it from a fixed sinker rig to a sliding sinker rig that allows fish to run with a bait on a free line.

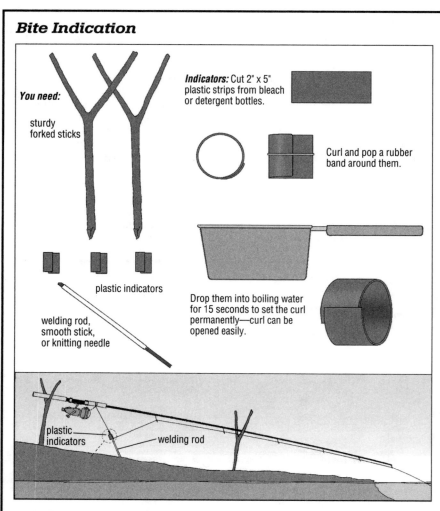

Bite Indication

You need:

sturdy forked sticks

Indicators: Cut 2" x 5" plastic strips from bleach or detergent bottles.

Curl and pop a rubber band around them.

plastic indicators

welding rod, smooth stick, or knitting needle

Drop them into boiling water for 15 seconds to set the curl permanently—curl can be opened easily.

plastic indicators   welding rod

1. Tighten line, engage reel, and lay rod in forked sticks.
2. Add one indicator to the line between the reel and first rod guide—pull the indicator almost to the ground.
3. Indicator rises to indicate a strike.
4. In wind, wrap several plastic indicators over each other to add weight; position the rod tip below the water so line doesn't blow around; slide an indicator on a rod inserted in the ground to keep the indicator from blowing around.
5. After a strike, remove the indicator with a flip of your fingers.

FISHING THE BASIC SET RIG

Where & When—Anytime you're targeting catfish, bullheads, or other fish that feed over relatively shallow, clean-bottom areas, this rig should be considered. It's certainly a top choice when fishing from shore. Set rigs excel when cast and anchored near an area likely to be inhabited by numbers of fish—at the top or bottom of a drop-off, a creek channel edge, or other high-percentage fish travel areas. The rig is highly susceptible to snags, however, so keep it out of sharp rocks, brush-piles, and heavy vegetation.

Presentation—As with most stationary rigs, successful presentation hinges on rig placement rather than how you manipulate the bait. Cast toward a likely spot, perhaps near cover, but not in cover. Place your rig and bait in the spot where a fish can find it. Once set in place, move the rig a few inches every ten minutes or so. This is especially important in rivers and other current areas. Your rig can drift into unfavorable spots, such as snags, where fish may not be able to find your bait. In some waters, crayfish, turtles, or small fish carry baits into rock crevices and other snags.

Whether fishing from shore or a boat, make your cast and, as the bait settles on the bottom, engage the reel then pick up slack until you're tight to the sinker. To detect bites, some anglers place the line over their index finger. Other times, particularly when fishing multiple rods, you can place rods into rod holders and use a bite indicator to detect light strikes. Common bite indicators include small bells attached to the rod tip, devices that signal a strike with a flashing light, or on-line indicators that drape over the line between guides. When a strike occurs, an on-line indicator rises or drops.

DROP-SHOT RIGGING

On a timeline of fishing rigs, the drop-shot is a new arrival. The rig traces its origins to Japan, where it was used to tempt highly selective large-mouth bass. Eventually, the drop-shot rig came to California, a state where finesse bass tactics are especially popular. Only recently has this presentation caught on with enthusiasts of other species. So while a drop-shot rig primarily teams with soft-plastic baits for large-mouth bass, it can easily be used with livebait for species like walleyes and crappies. The rig can also be coupled with different sizes and styles of plastic baits for smallmouth bass, bluegills, and white bass.

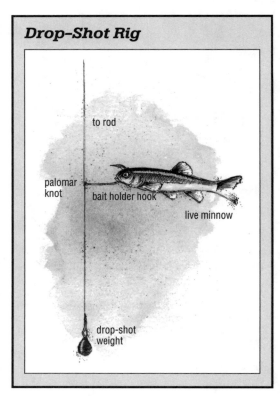

Drop-Shot Rig

to rod

palomar knot

bait holder hook

live minnow

drop-shot weight

As more anglers begin modifying drop-shot rigs for use in new situations, they will continue to catch more fish of all species. The beauty of the drop-shot rig lies in its adaptability as well as its unique functionality. It fills a niche in a universe of diverse fishing situations. Specifically, the drop-shot rig places a bait at a set distance above bottom, moving it almost perfectly horizontal through the water.

PRIMARY SPECIES

TACKLE

Rod & Reel—A 6- to 7-foot moderately-fast-action, medium-power spinning rod; a medium-capacity spinning reel.

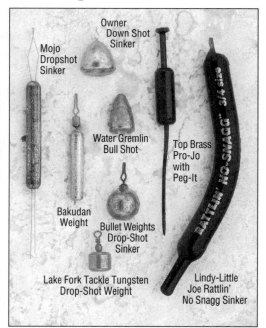

Sinker Options

Owner
Down Shot
Sinker

Mojo
Dropshot
Sinker

Water Gremlin
Bull Shot

Top Brass
Pro-Jo
with
Peg-It

Bakudan
Weight

Bullet Weights
Drop-Shot
Sinker

Lake Fork Tackle Tungsten
Drop-Shot Weight

RATTLIN' NO-SNAGG™ 3/4 size

Lindy-Little
Joe Rattlin'
No Snagg Sinker

Consider sinker weight first, though shape, rigging attachments, and material also are important. For anchoring a rig, choose a heavy weight like a special drop-shot weight or a bell sinker. Lighter weights feather the bottom for a smooth drift. In snaggy conditions, use elongated weights. Tungsten is the densest sinker material, followed by lead, Ultra Steel 2000, brass, and tin.

Line—Since drop-shotting typically is used in clear water, most anglers use 4- to 8-pound monofilament or fluorocarbon line. Go heavier for larger fish and larger baits. Some anglers prefer ultrathin 8-pound fused superlines, which impart extra action to soft plastics and deliver solid hooksets.

Sinker—Like the set rig, the drop-shot rig positions the weight at the base of the rig, while the hook is fastened to the line above the sinker. Many sinker designs work, though the simplest solution is to pinch a split shot on the end of the line. This allows a snagged sinker to pull free from the line, rather that breaking off the rig. Other anglers peg a sliding bullet sinker in place with a piece of rubberband. Bullet weights resist snagging in weeds, brush, and wood. Specialized drop-shot weights sport special line-gripping eyes. Tie an overhand knot at the end of the line, run it through the eye, and snag the knot against the eye to hold the weight in place.

Hook Choices

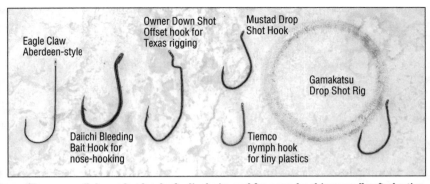

Choose small drop-shot hooks for livebaits and for nose-hooking small soft plastics. The largest hooks are reserved for Texas-rigging shad baits or tubes. The hooks featured here are examples of hook styles to consider for this presentation.

Connections—No swivels required.

Knots—To make a plastic bait ride horizontally on the line, a palomar knot is critical. Once you've cinched the knot tight, the hook will stick out straight (perpendicular) from the line, hook point up. Remember to leave a long tag end beyond the hook, which serves as the dropper for attaching a sinker. The length of the tag determines the distance between bait and sinker, and the distance the bait rides above bottom. Common dropper lengths run from 6 inches to 6 feet.

Hooks—Small plastic baits used on this finesse rig call for light-wire hooks. When fishing near cover for bass, Texas-rig plastic baits with a #1 to 2/0 wide-gap offset hook. Away from cover, use short-shank #4 to 2/0 bait-style hooks. Insert the hook up through the nose of the bait, exposing

Plastic Bait Options

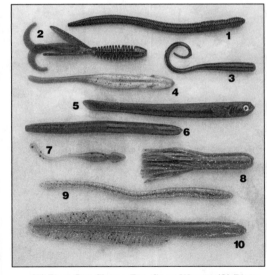

(1) Bass Pro Shops Eco Gear Worm; (2) Riverside Woolly Hawg; (3) Berkley Bungee Worm; (4) SnakeBite Super Jerk; (5) AA Shiner; (6) Mann's Dragin' Finesse; (7) No Name Tsuchinoko; (8) Midsouth MST; (9) Western Hand Pour Finesse Worm; (10) Dezyner Cow Tongue.

the point. For smaller 1- to 3-inch panfish plastics, use a similar #10 to #6 hook. These same light-wire short-shank hooks can be used for livebait.

Soft Plastics—Small subtle plastics most commonly are used on drop-shot rigs. Reapers, swimming minnows, and finesse and do-nothing-style worms produce many species of fish, including largemouth bass. For bass, opt for 3- to 6-inch baits. For panfish, use 1- to 4-inchers. As the drop-shot rig is simply a bait delivery system, any size or style of soft plastic concoction will potentially work. Remember, though, that as target fish and bait size increase, so should terminal tackle and rod and reel selection, matching tackle to the situation at hand.

Natural Baits—Choose small- to medium-sized baits, such as 1- to 4-inch shiners, chubs, ribbon leeches, nightcrawlers, angleworms, or insect larva.

RIGGING WRINKLES

One effective modification is the addition of a second (or third) hook and bait farther up or down the line. Perhaps you're trying to pinpoint the exact depth of a pod of crappies. Attach one hook with a small minnow 3 feet above the sinker, then another hook 12 inches above the sinker. This is just one of many possible combinations. Consider other bait options, too, such as marabou flies.

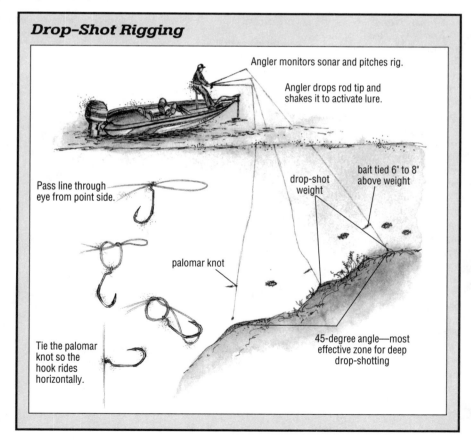

Drop-Shot Rigging

Angler monitors sonar and pitches rig.

Angler drops rod tip and shakes it to activate lure.

Pass line through eye from point side.

bait tied 6" to 8" above weight

drop-shot weight

palomar knot

Tie the palomar knot so the hook rides horizontally.

45-degree angle—most effective zone for deep drop-shotting

FISHING THE DROP-SHOT RIG

Where & When—Use this rig primarily for fishing nearly vertical beneath a boat. It's not a search lure—one to help you find fish—but rather a rig that shines when fished in small areas known to attract fish. Generally, think late spring through fall; clear water deeper than 12 to 15 feet, and areas lacking dense cover, like flooded brush or thick weeds. Drop-shot rigs excel for suspended, heavily pressured fish.

Presentation—Fishing a drop-shot rig is a lot like fishing a Carolina rig, only slower and more meticulous, almost like vertical jigging. That's the reason the rig works so well; it caters to sluggish or pressured fish. The little plastic bait hovers in place, shaking and quivering above bottom just like a live critter. Eventually, a fish simply has to eat it.

Not only is the rig effective, but it's also simple to fish. Anglers of all skill levels enjoy fishing a drop-shot rig. Make a short cast, 30 feet or less. Let the rig fall straight to the bottom. Your line should hang at a 45-degree angle to the water, becoming steeper as the bait is retrieved toward the boat. Drop the rod to about 10 o'clock and shake the rod tip slowly and deliberately. Don't overwork the bait. Rather, give it just enough action to make it look alive. Let the sinker sit in the same spot on bottom for several seconds, often longer, before retrieving the rig a few feet.

As an alternative to casting, slowly drift while dragging the rig along bottom, occasionally twitching the rod to make the bait dance. This works best in deeper water, at least 15 feet, where you can hover above the fish without spooking them.

Sliding Sinker Rigs

THE SLIPSINKER REVOLUTION

Teamed with livebait, the slipsinker rig has accounted for more walleyes than any other presentation. But the slipsinker rig is versatile enough to catch all fish species, not just walleyes.

The heart of the rig is the sinker sliding on the line above a swivel. Teamed with a healthy, actively swimming baitfish, leech, worm, or other livebait, this rig accounts for mixed bags of fish throughout the season.

PRIMARY SPECIES

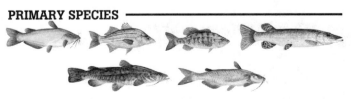

TACKLE

Rod & Reel—A 7- to 10-foot medium-action, medium-power spinning or casting rod; a medium-capacity spinning or casting reel.

Line—6- to 10-pound-test monofilament or fused superline.

Sinker—A 1/8- to 3/4-ounce walking or egg sinker for fishing over sand, gravel, and small rock; a bullet sinker for weeds and wood; and a bell or bass casting sinker for holding bottom in moderate current.

Sinker placement determines bait action. The closer you place the sinker to the hook, the more control you have over bait movement and action, though the bait is given less freedom to swim. Conversely, a sinker removed from the bait by 4 feet or more allows the bait a wider range of movement, potentially triggering more fish.

Some anglers believe that using a colored sinker adds a bit of appeal to their rig, but this remains largely unproven. It rarely hurts to try, though, since the added color might attract fish to your bait.

Connections—A small barrel swivel or ball-bearing swivel connects the leader to the main line.

Leader—Use a 1- to 6-foot section of 4- to 10-pound-test monofilament or fluorocarbon. Active fish, or fish holding close to bottom call for a short snell—1 to 3 feet. Pressured or slightly suspended fish and clear water often call for longer snells—4- to 10-footers.

Rig Advantages / Disadvantages

Slipsinker Rig	Advantages	Disadvantages
Presents livebait and deadbait.	Natural presentation when worked slowly.	Sinker tends to snag in rocks.
	Presents large livebaits effectively.	Rig flattens to bottom in current.
	Effective in deep water.	Must be presented slowly to be effective.
	Good for neutral and negative fish.	

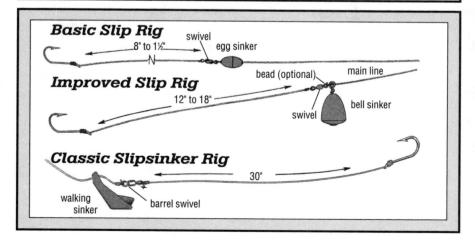

Basic Slip Rig
swivel
8" to 1½" egg sinker

Improved Slip Rig
bead (optional) main line
12" to 18"
bell sinker
swivel

Classic Slipsinker Rig
30"
walking sinker barrel swivel

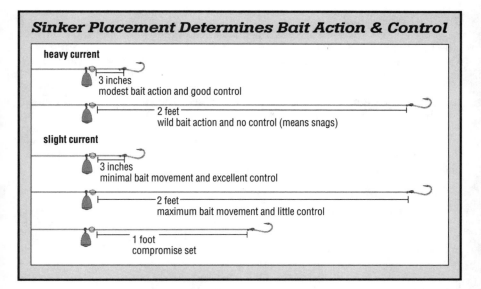

Sinker Placement Determines Bait Action & Control

heavy current

3 inches
modest bait action and good control

2 feet
wild bait action and no control (means snags)

slight current

3 inches
minimal bait movement and excellent control

2 feet
maximum bait movement and little control

1 foot
compromise set

Knots—Attach the leader to the hook with a snell knot when using hooks with up-turned or down-turned eyes. Other line connections should be made with a Trilene knot.

Hooks—Choose #2 to 1/0 octopus or wide-gap hooks for 3- to 6-inch minnows and amphibians; #6 to #8 octopus hooks for leeches, and #4 to #8 octopus or baitholder hooks for nightcrawlers. It's vital to use super-sharp hooks. Use premium hooks, or use a hook hone to touch up hook points.

Natural Baits—When using livebait always use the liveliest, healthiest critters available. Use the minnow that's toughest to catch or the strongest-swimming leech in your baitwell. Top-producing baits include ribbon leeches, nightcrawlers, fathead minnows, shiners, redtail chubs, redbelly dace, white suckers, leopard frogs, waterdogs, and crayfish.

While backtrolling or moving slowly along structure, hook a minnow through the jaws or into the mouth and out lightly through a nostril. When hovering in place, try reverse rigging. Leeches work best when hooked once just behind the sucker. When using crawlers, run the hook once through the head. Or try the opposite to show the fish a slightly different look. Other effective natural baits include cutbait, particularly f or channel and blue catfish. In certain situations, whole dead minnows also produce.

Reverse Rigging

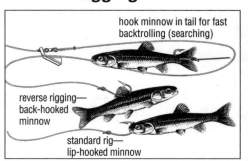

hook minnow in tail for fast backtrolling (searching)

reverse rigging—
back-hooked
minnow

standard rig—
lip-hooked minnow

The farther back the hook is placed in the bone, the less likely the minnow is to come loose, but the less action it will have. Insert a hook with a file-reduced barb, just into the beginning of the bone structure in the minnow's top jaw.

RIGGING WRINKLES

Many anglers add a colored plastic bead ahead of the hook, hoping to attract attention to the bait. Certain beads also float. By employing either a floating bead ahead of the hook or swapping the hook for a floating jighead, the livebait rises slightly above bottom where fish more likely will see your offering.

In addition to beads and floats, some situations necessitate spinner blades in combination with beads. Spinner snells work best when pulled along bottom at a slightly faster speed.

Another enhancement of the slipsinker rig is a sinker stop. The beauty of the stop is that it allows you to instantly adjust leader length by sliding the stop in either direction. The stop is either a tiny neoprene bead or a stop knot tied with Dacron line. Position the stop and a plastic bead between the sinker and the stop knot.

FISHING A SLIPSINKER RIG

Where & When—This rig excels when fish group into relatively small areas or travel along a specific contour on a well-defined break. Consider it anytime fish aren't feeding aggressively, but it can be triggered to strike the right bait placed in front of their noses. Slipsinker rigs are most popular among walleye fishermen in natural lakes and catfish anglers using livebait or cutbait in rivers.

Presentation—A slipsinker rig can be cast and slowly retrieved along bottom. It also works as a set rig, cast and set in place near key spots in lakes, reservoirs, and rivers. The classic presentation method, though, is fishing it vertically below a slow-moving boat. The boat becomes part of the presentation, as boat movement controls the retrieve.

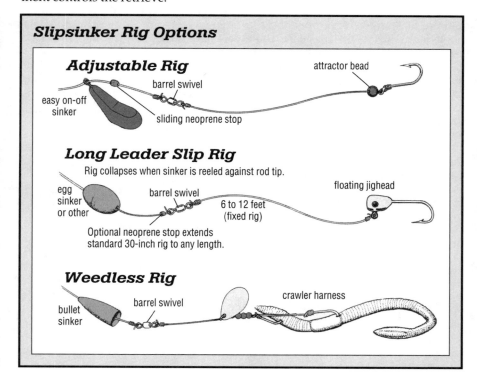

Slipsinker Rig Options

Adjustable Rig

attractor bead

barrel swivel

easy on-off sinker

sliding neoprene stop

Long Leader Slip Rig

Rig collapses when sinker is reeled against rod tip.

floating jighead

egg sinker or other

barrel swivel

6 to 12 feet (fixed rig)

Optional neoprene stop extends standard 30-inch rig to any length.

Weedless Rig

crawler harness

bullet sinker

barrel swivel

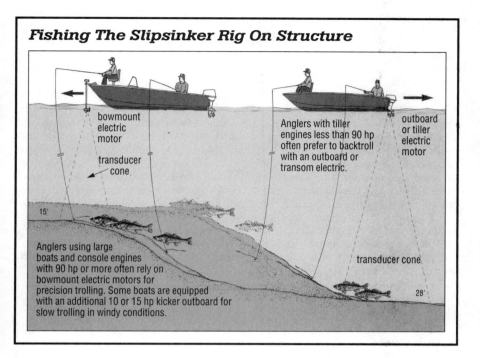

Fishing The Slipsinker Rig On Structure

bowmount
electric
motor

transducer
cone

Anglers with tiller
engines less than 90 hp
often prefer to backtroll
with an outboard or
transom electric.

outboard
or tiller
electric
motor

15'

Anglers using large
boats and console engines
with 90 hp or more often rely on
bowmount electric motors for
precision trolling. Some boats are equipped
with an additional 10 or 15 hp kicker outboard for
slow trolling in windy conditions.

transducer cone

28'

CAROLINA RIGGING

As the popularity of finesse tactics has grown, so has the Carolina rig. This was first popularized in 1985 by tournament angler Jack Chancellor, who Carolina-rigged a straight "do-nothing" worm to win the Bassmasters Classic. Plastic baits trail well behind the sinker on a leader, giving fish a subtle offering. Unencumbered by weight (other than the hook), the bait freely darts, flutters, rises, or hovers as the angler imparts rod action. But the rig isn't just for bass. With a bit of alteration, a Carolina rig can just as easily present plastics or livebait to walleyes, pike, panfish, and many other species. The fun's learning how different fish react to each new variation, given each bait's unique profile and action.

PRIMARY SPECIES _____

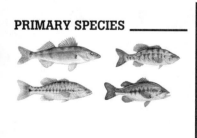

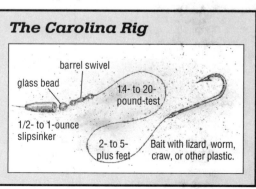

The Carolina Rig

barrel swivel

glass bead

14- to 20-
pound-test

1/2- to 1-ounce
slipsinker

2- to 5-
plus feet

Bait with lizard, worm,
craw, or other plastic.

TACKLE

Rod & Reel—A 6½- to 7-foot moderately-fast-action, medium-heavy-power casting rod; medium-capacity casting reel.

Line—12- to 14-pound-test, abrasion-resistant monofilament. In heavier cover, consider fused superline or 17- to 20-pound-test monofilament.

Sinker—Most anglers use a 1/2- to 1-ounce bullet sinker that slides on the line. Modern Carolina riggers also often opt for brass sinkers over lead, which produces louder "clacks" when contacting rocks or wood, better attracting the attention of fish.

Connections—A barrel swivel is standard, separating the weight from the lure and reducing line twist. One or more plastic or glass beads slides on the line between sinker and swivel to protect the knot and produce subtle clicking sounds.

Leader—Typical leader lengths range from 1 to 4 feet, although longer snells up to 7 feet allow plastic baits a greater range of movement. Choose longer leaders when fishing in areas lacking snaggy cover and when dealing with inactive fish. Conversely, shorter leaders allow better control over the lure. One- to three-footers work best when dealing with heavy cover or fish lying tight to the bottom.

Match leader material to the conditions. In heavy cover, stay with 14- to 20-pound-test, abrasion-resistant monofilament. In clear water and on heavily pressured fish, fluorocarbon leaders are a good choice.

Carolina Rigging Rattlers

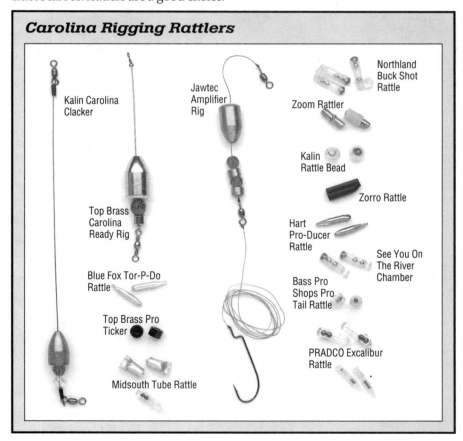

Kalin Carolina Clacker

Jawtec Amplifier Rig

Northland Buck Shot Rattle

Zoom Rattler

Kalin Rattle Bead

Zorro Rattle

Top Brass Carolina Ready Rig

Hart Pro-Ducer Rattle

See You On The River Chamber

Blue Fox Tor-P-Do Rattle

Bass Pro Shops Pro Tail Rattle

Top Brass Pro Ticker

PRADCO Excalibur Rattle

Midsouth Tube Rattle

Knots—Palomar or Trilene knots yield strong connections on leaders and hooks.

Hooks—Selecting the right hook means first choosing the lure. A standard choice for rigging 6-inch worms or lizards is a 2/0 to 4/0 wide-gap worm hook. To produce a plastic or natural bait that floats above bottom, you'll need to rig the bait on a floating jighead or add an in-line float.

Soft Plastics—The first Carolina rigs incorporated 6- to 7-inch soft plastic lizards. Many anglers also opt for 6- to 8-inch curlytail worms. Each year, though, dozens of new shapes, sizes, and colors of plastic baits are introduced. In addition to classic worms and lizards, swimming worms, straight or finesse worms, tubes, and other creatures all produce. Carry floating and sinking baits; both presentations excel, at times. Floating baits often produce best, though, because they hover above cover and remain more visible to bass.

Natural Baits—Carolina rigs efficiently present livebaits, too. Top options include hardy baits that can be repeatedly cast and retrieved, including 4- to 8-inch chubs, suckers, crayfish, waterdogs, and nightcrawlers.

RIGGING WRINKLES

Various sinker and bead combinations produce audible clicking sounds as they contact each other or solid objects on the bottom. Several companies offer glass or plastic rattle chambers filled with BBs that produce additional noise during the retrieve. Another wrinkle incorporates a neoprene stop or Dacron stop knot between the sinker and the swivel. This transforms the rig into one that yields instant adjustments in leader length. Finally, try a Mojo Rig, which offers many Carolina rig advantages but is more flexible in some situations.

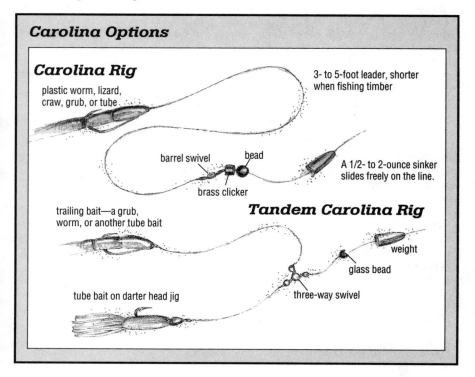

Carolina Options

Carolina Rig

plastic worm, lizard, craw, grub, or tube

3- to 5-foot leader, shorter when fishing timber

barrel swivel
bead
brass clicker

A 1/2- to 2-ounce sinker slides freely on the line.

trailing bait—a grub, worm, or another tube bait

Tandem Carolina Rig

weight
glass bead
three-way swivel

tube bait on darter head jig

Mojo Rig—A Variation

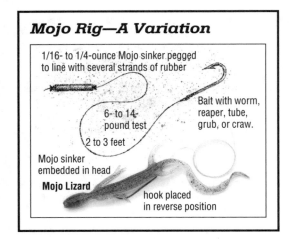

1/16- to 1/4-ounce Mojo sinker pegged to line with several strands of rubber

6- to 14-pound test

2 to 3 feet

Bait with worm, reaper, tube, grub, or craw.

Mojo sinker embedded in head

Mojo Lizard

hook placed in reverse position

FISHING THE CAROLINA RIG

Where & When—Carolina-rigged baits produce shallow-water bass and other fish holding tight to cover, but they really shine in deeper water—deeper than 10 feet—away from dense vegetation or woodcover. Carolina rigging is most effective in lakes and reservoirs with clean-bottomed points, sunken islands, and other deep-water habitat. It's also a method that works throughout summer, fall, and winter, or whenever fish use deep-water structure.

Presentation—Casting a Carolina rig is similar to casting a bobber rig. Swing the entire rig to the side and behind you by holding the rod at roughly 10 o'clock while waving it sideways like a wand. To finish the cast, swing the rod toward the target, propelling the rig as if releasing a pendulum.

Retrieve the Carolina rig with slow, intermittent drags along the bottom. Sweep the bait a foot forward, pause, and then sweep it forward again with a sideways pull of the rod. Use shorter rod movements when working smaller areas or targeting less aggressive fish. When the sinker is dragged along bottom, a floating bait scoots forward—like a helium balloon dragged downward when pulled behind you on a string. At rest, the lure, like the balloon, slowly ascends until the sinker stops it. Not all plastic baits float, however, so it's important to determine the lure's buoyancy prior to your first cast. And though most Carolina rigging situations call for a floating bait, sometimes a sinking lure works better. Think of the critter you're trying to imitate. If it's a minnow, go with a floater, if it's a crayfish, use a sinking bait.

TEXAS RIG

Texas-rigged plastic worms probably have accounted for more bass than any other lure. During the late 1950s and 1960s, when the rig burst onto the southern bass scene, fishermen were astounded by their newfound success. In the years since, developments in soft plastics, including new colors, sizes, shapes, scents, and flavors, have continually kept things fresh, not to mention staying a step ahead of increasingly "educated" fish.

While action-packed plastics keep bass interested, they'd be worthless without a functional rig. The Texas rig works because it fishes like a dream, slithering easily through the densest cover—weeds, brush, and timber. With many species, not just bass, the thickest cover holds the biggest fish.

PRIMARY SPECIES

TACKLE

Rod & Reel—A 6½- to 7½-foot fast-action, medium-heavy-power casting rod or heavy-power flipping stick for especially heavy cover; medium-capacity casting reel equipped with a flipping switch.

Line—17- to 30-pound-test, abrasion-resistant monofilament.

Sinker—The bullet-shaped slipsinker plays an integral role in this rigging scheme. A 1/8- to 1-ounce bullet weight slides on the line above the bait. The streamlined shape slides easily through obstructions. A common practice is to poke the tip of a wooden toothpick into the head of the sinker, then break it off at the hole. This pins the sinker tightly to the hook, preventing it from separating from the bait, which might cause snags. The sinker and worm present fish with a seamless "package" of food. They probably see the sinker and lure as one single item, rather than separately, as is the case with a Carolina rig.

Knots—Standard terminal connections, such as the Trilene knot, are appropriate.

Hooks—Consider two general hook styles: straight-shank worm hooks with barbs near the eye to hold plastics in place, or offset hooks that secure the head of the plastic in the shank bend. Once you've selected the right hook, the most important consideration becomes matching hook size and gap to the type and thickness of the bait. Thicker-bodied plastics and tubes call for a wide-gap hook. With thinner plastic worms, a narrower hook gap works fine. An assortment of hooks from #1 to 5/0 will cover most Texas-rigging options. For 6- to 8-inch worms, choose a 2/0 to 4/0 hook.

Sinker Styles

Standard Lead

Thunder Bullets Bait Lock

Bullet Weights UltraSteel

Top Brass

Gambler Rat'lin Florida Rig

Top Brass Carolina Quake

Gambler Carolina Weight

Jawtec Brass

Lunker City Lunker Grip

Thunder Bullets Brass N' Bullets

Kicker Rig

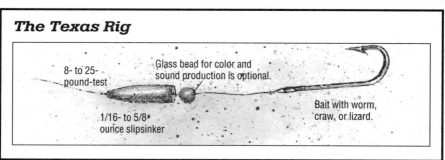

The Texas Rig

8- to 25-pound-test

Glass bead for color and sound production is optional.

Bait with worm, craw, or lizard.

1/16- to 5/8-ounce slipsinker

Texas rigging begins by inserting the hook point into the tip of the worm's head and threading it down 1/4 inch or so, then poking it back out of the body. Now, pull the worm up the shank until the head rests against the eye. Rotate the hook 180 degrees so the hook points toward the plastic. Most worms have straight seams on each side; use a seam to rig the worm straight. Bunch the worm toward the eye a bit and insert the hook back into the worm, burying the point in the soft plastic body. The worm should have no kink, for kinked worms tend to twirl in the water, twisting your line and turning fish off. Rigged right, there's not a more snagless, weedless lure in existence.

Soft Plastics—The universal bait for Texas rigging remains the curlytail plastic worm, but almost any soft plastic bait will work. Lizards, reapers, crayfish, grubs, even tubes—all team well with Texas rigging. The challenge lies in matching the right plastic concoction to the situation.

Natural Baits—This is one of the few rigging options that doesn't work well with most natural baits. The way a bait must be hooked to fish weedless kills livebaits. The one exception is a large nightcrawler, which can be rigged exactly like a soft-plastic imitation.

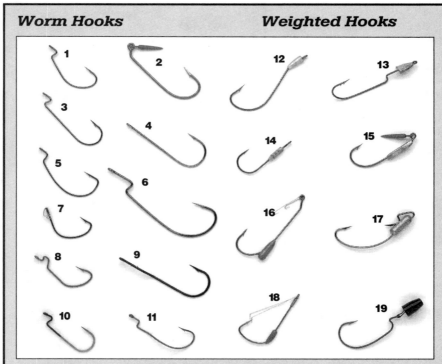

Worm Hooks   Weighted Hooks

(1) Owner J Hook; (2) Mister Twister Smart Hook; (3) Offset Shank VMC; (4) Mustad Flippin' Hook; (5) Gamakatsu EWG; (6) Owner Oversize (11/00); (7) Luck "E" Strike HP; (8) Eagle Claw R Bend Featherlite; (9) Tru-Turn; (10) Berkley Gold Point; (11) Eagle Claw Messler; (12) Blue Fox Hidden Head; (13) Eagle Claw LT95; (14) M & N Weighted Hook; (15) Mister Twister Swimmin Smart Hook; (16) Mustad Needle Power Lock; (17) VMC Z-Gap; (18) Mustad Fin-A'cky; (19) Bullet Weights Ultra Jigging System.

FISHING THE TEXAS RIG

Where & When—Anytime you're targeting fish relating to or buried in heavy cover, the Texas rig shines. It penetrates the most inaccessible haunts imaginable, going where few lures can go.

Because the Texas rig is a subtle rig that's fished slowly, choose it whenever fish, particularly bass, display a neutral to slightly negative attitude. Less aggressive, pressured, or semi-spooked fish often tuck down below thick weed clumps or brushpiles, under docks, or lie at the base of timber. Because the lure works best within a foot of bottom and is probably the most weedless lure ever devised, it's a great choice for these situations.

Presentation—Short casts or flips work best for working small areas around cover objects or general high-percentage zones. Generally, fishing a Texas-rigged worm involves many of the same mechanics as jigs. The slow lift-drop-pause appeals to most fish.

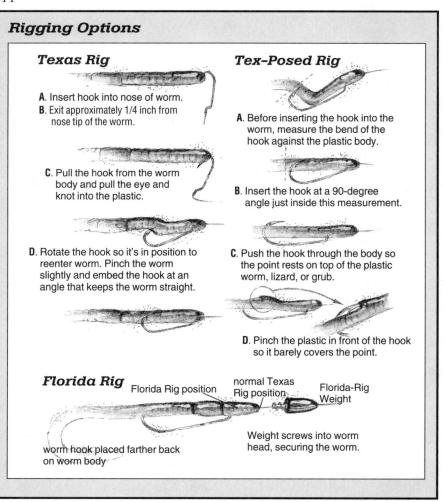

Rigging Options

Texas Rig

A. Insert hook into nose of worm.
B. Exit approximately 1/4 inch from nose tip of the worm.

C. Pull the hook from the worm body and pull the eye and knot into the plastic.

D. Rotate the hook so it's in position to reenter worm. Pinch the worm slightly and embed the hook at an angle that keeps the worm straight.

Tex-Posed Rig

A. Before inserting the hook into the worm, measure the bend of the hook against the plastic body.

B. Insert the hook at a 90-degree angle just inside this measurement.

C. Push the hook through the body so the point rests on top of the plastic worm, lizard, or grub.

D. Pinch the plastic in front of the hook so it barely covers the point.

Florida Rig

Florida Rig position

normal Texas Rig position

Florida-Rig Weight

Weight screws into worm head, securing the worm.

worm hook placed farther back on worm body

Trolling Rigs

MAINTAINING SPEED AND DEPTH CONTROL

First conceived by tackle maker Bob Meter over 30 years ago in the Missouri River region of the Dakotas, the idea for these odd-shaped contraptions resulted from a need to cover expansive rock- and snag-encrusted flats. Although traditional livebait rigging caught fish, walleye anglers in this region needed a way to present livebaits, such as nightcrawlers, with a bit more speed, while keeping their sinkers from snagging in rocks.

PRIMARY SPECIES

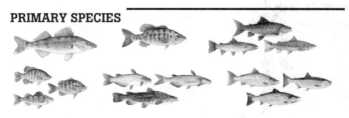

TACKLE

Rod & Reel—A 6- to 7-foot moderately-fast-action, medium-power casting rod; medium-capacity casting reel, preferably equipped with a flipping switch.

Line—10-pound-test, abrasion-resistant monofilament.

Sinker—The impetus of the rig, the bottom bouncer, is an upside-down section of L-shaped wire fastened to a cylindrical piece of lead. Common weights vary from 1/2 to 2 ounces. The wire feeler arm ticks along uneven bottoms, particularly rocks, rarely snagging. The main line attaches to a twist or an eye at the bend in the wire, while a leader trails behind a snap swivel tethered to the short arm.

Leader—The usual accompaniment to a bottom bouncer is a spinner rig and crawler harness. This is far from a rule, though, as many anglers employ other livebaits and rigging schemes behind a bouncer with much success. Plain-hook minnow rigs, a single bead and a leech, even light spoons or shallow-diving minnowbaits produce plenty of fish.

From left to right, popular bottom bouncers include the Northland Rock Runner; Bait Rigs Bottom Bouncer; Quick Change Lite Bite Slip Bouncer; and Lindy-Little Joe Bottom Cruiser. The final option is the Angling Jenny.

The standard spinner rig uses a 1½- to 3-foot leader and a #2 to #4 Colorado blade, fastened by a clevis, in front of three to six colored beads. Surprisingly, bead color may be more visible to fish than blade color, which often blurs while rotating. Many commercially produced spinner rigs are available, though many anglers prefer the flexibility of customizing their own rigs, incorporating a multitude of blade, clevis, bead, and hook combinations. Generally, active fish lying on snaggy bottoms call for shorter leaders.

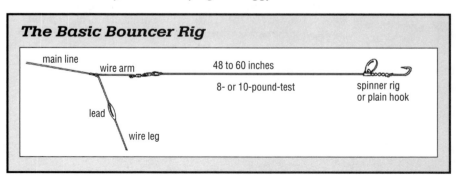

The Basic Bouncer Rig

main line

wire arm

48 to 60 inches

8- or 10-pound-test

spinner rig or plain hook

lead

wire leg

Bouncer Advantages / Disadvantages

Bottom Bouncer	Advantages	Disadvantages
Presents livebait, floaters, spinners, and crankbaits.	Ideal for covering water quickly Snag resistant. Adjusts depth as it crawls over dips and rises.	Less effective than slipsinker rig for slow, vertical presentations. Less effective in deep water (30 feet plus). Unnecessary when fish are tightly concentrated.

Short leaders sag less than long leaders behind a bottom bouncer, making them less likely to hang up. Inactive or pressured fish, or fish spread over clean sand or mudflats, sometimes call for longer leaders.

Knots—A snell knot makes the critical link between hook and leader, providing a strong and reliable connection.

Hooks—When using crawlers, a tandem in-line "harness" consisting of two #4 or #6 baitholder hooks works best. The barbs on baitholders secure nightcrawlers in place. Some harnesses replace the tail baitholder with a #6 or #8 treble hook, which allows for instant hooksets. When using leeches or minnows, a single octopus or wide-gap hook works best. Some minnow rigs also require a #2 to 1/0 Aberdeen.

Natural Baits—Hook nightcrawlers, leeches, and minnows so they trail straight and natural behind a trolled bottom bouncer. A harnessed crawler should first be hooked lightly through the head. Stretch the crawler out to its full length and insert the tail hook into the body so the worm doesn't kink or spin. When the crawler contracts its body, the line between the two hooks should slacken.

For leeches, insert the hook just behind the sucker. Minnows can be hooked

Common Spinner Rig

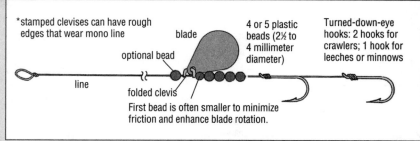

*stamped clevises can have rough edges that wear mono line

blade

optional bead

line

folded clevis

First bead is often smaller to minimize friction and enhance blade rotation.

4 or 5 plastic beads (2½ to 4 millimeter diameter)

Turned-down-eye hooks: 2 hooks for crawlers; 1 hook for leeches or minnows

Spinners are the most popular modification of livebait rigs. Spinner blades typically rotate on a clevis ahead of crawlers, minnows, or leeches. A set of beads maintains adequate distance between the clevis and bait to allow the blade to spin without striking the hook. Beads also add bulk and a splash of color to the rig. Vary bead size and number for different effects.

Blade Angle Determines Action

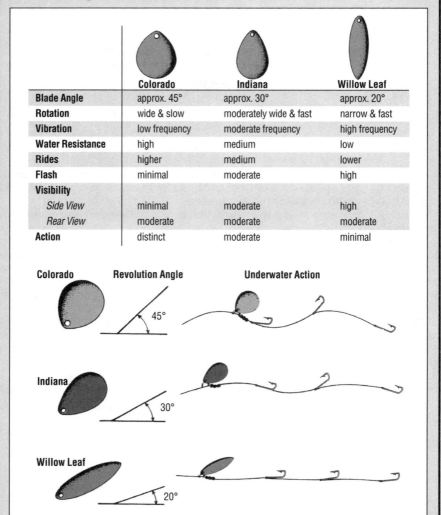

	Colorado	Indiana	Willow Leaf
Blade Angle	approx. 45°	approx. 30°	approx. 20°
Rotation	wide & slow	moderately wide & fast	narrow & fast
Vibration	low frequency	moderate frequency	high frequency
Water Resistance	high	medium	low
Rides	higher	medium	lower
Flash	minimal	moderate	high
Visibility			
Side View	minimal	moderate	high
Rear View	moderate	moderate	moderate
Action	distinct	moderate	minimal

Colorado   **Revolution Angle**   **Underwater Action**

45°

Indiana

30°

Willow Leaf

20°

Action is determined by blade shape and the angle of revolution. Wider blade revolutions produce more action.

Spinner blades come in three popular configurations, though others are used as well. Colorado (wide) blades have a wide angle of rotation and spin at low speeds. Indiana (intermediate) blades rotate at a shallower angle and require slightly more speed to spin properly. Long, thin willow leaf blades rotate on a tight axis and require the most forward speed to make them spin. Willows give off the most flash, Colorados the most noticeable vibration, with Indianas exhibiting characteristics of both. Sizes #2 through #5 Colorados and Indianas are most popular.

Hooking For Bouncer Rigging

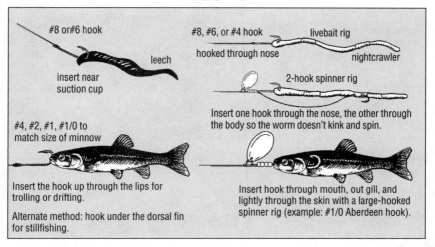

#8 or#6 hook

leech

insert near suction cup

#8, #6, or #4 hook — livebait rig
hooked through nose — nightcrawler

2-hook spinner rig

Insert one hook through the nose, the other through the body so the worm doesn't kink and spin.

#4, #2, #1, #1/0 to match size of minnow

Insert the hook up through the lips for trolling or drifting.

Alternate method: hook under the dorsal fin for stillfishing.

Insert hook through mouth, out gill, and lightly through the skin with a large-hooked spinner rig (example: #1/0 Aberdeen hook).

once through the bottom lip and out the top lip. Or to hook minnows more securely, insert an aberdeen hook through the mouth and out a gill, being careful not to pierce any tissue, then turn the hook and lightly penetrate the skin near the dorsal fin. Done properly, the minnow will trail perfectly straight.

Artificial Baits—Shallow-diving minnowbaits, trolled on a 2- to 3-foot leader, effectively take many fish species including walleyes, trout, and salmon. Light flutterspoons also troll well behind a bottom bouncer.

RIGGING WRINKLES

Each year manufacturers introduce new products worth trying—floating spinners, rattling beads, colored hooks, and quick-change clevises. Creative do-it-yourself spinner-makers relish that with a supply of components, an infinite number of rigging combinations exist. The next rig you tie could be the hot combination.

FISHING A BOTTOM BOUNCER

Where & When—Bottom bouncers work well when increased speed (relative to slower slipsinker rigging) is necessary. This rig remains a wonderful tool for locating fish scattered across large areas, without moving too fast. Bouncers excel over sharp rock bottoms, remaining largely snag-free. Whenever fish like walleyes or trout spread out on flats, but are holding within a foot or so of the bottom, trolling a bottom bouncer and spinner rig scores big.

Speed—From as slow as a 1/2 mph drift to 3 mph while trolling.

Presentation—Anglers commonly talk about "power trolling" with bottom bouncers. Power trolling simply means moving along at a fair clip, say 1½ mph, while pulling a bottom bouncer rig at roughly a 45-degree angle to the boat. The wire feeler-arm ticks across bottom while a leader trails behind. Drop the rig straight to the bottom and begin drifting or trolling. When you detect a strike, drop the rod tip back several feet, then throw a deep arc into the rod. Fish that hit a trolled bouncer rig usually are aggressive. No need to wait long on the hookset.

Bouncers For Dragging

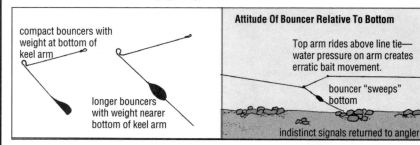

compact bouncers with weight at bottom of keel arm

longer bouncers with weight nearer bottom of keel arm

Attitude Of Bouncer Relative To Bottom

Top arm rides above line tie—water pressure on arm creates erratic bait movement.

bouncer "sweeps" bottom

indistinct signals returned to angler

Dragging

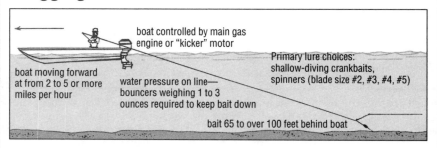

boat controlled by main gas engine or "kicker" motor

boat moving forward at from 2 to 5 or more miles per hour

water pressure on line—bouncers weighing 1 to 3 ounces required to keep bait down

Primary lure choices: shallow-diving crankbaits, spinners (blade size #2, #3, #4, #5)

bait 65 to over 100 feet behind boat

The Precision Bouncer

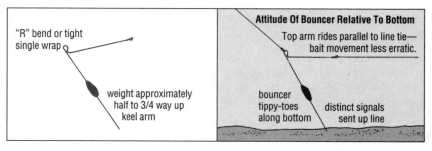

"R" bend or tight single wrap

weight approximately half to 3/4 way up keel arm

Attitude Of Bouncer Relative To Bottom

Top arm rides parallel to line tie—bait movement less erratic.

bouncer tippy-toes along bottom

distinct signals sent up line

The Precision Bouncer

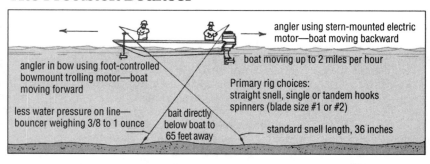

angler using stern-mounted electric motor—boat moving backward

boat moving up to 2 miles per hour

angler in bow using foot-controlled bowmount trolling motor—boat moving forward

less water pressure on line—bouncer weighing 3/8 to 1 ounce

bait directly below boat to 65 feet away

Primary rig choices: straight snell, single or tandem hooks spinners (blade size #1 or #2)

standard snell length, 36 inches

THREE-WAY RIGGING

The old Wolf River rig, the forerunner of what today is referred to as a three-way rig, was originally designed to present livebait just off river bottoms where fish could easily see it. News flash: The rig isn't just for rivers anymore. Truth is, it never was, though it does excel in current. Three-ways aren't even exclusively trolling rigs, as they can be adapted to present static natural baits for fish like catfish and steelhead in lakes, rivers, and reservoirs.

PRIMARY SPECIES

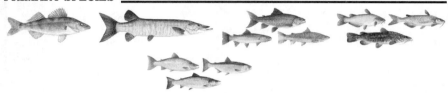

TACKLE

Rod & Reel—A moderate- to fast-action, medium- to heavy-power casting rod, 6½ to 7½ feet long, depending on sinker weight and target fish species; medium-capacity casting reel, preferably equipped with a flipping switch for instant line release. A line-counting reel might be helpful for trolling.

Line—Main line: 10- to 20-pound fused superline for plugs or spoons, mono for livebait rigs. Wire line is often used for deep-water trolling, particularly for salmon, lake trout, and muskies. Dropper line: A 1- to 3-foot section of 8- to 12-pound, abrasion-resistant monofilament works well for sinker droppers. Dropper length varies according to how far fish lie off bottom. Anglers working the rig in snag-filled areas often use a lighter line on the dropper than for the leader or main line. If they hit a snag, they pull until the dropper breaks off, leaving the rest of the rig intact.

Standard Three-Way Rigging

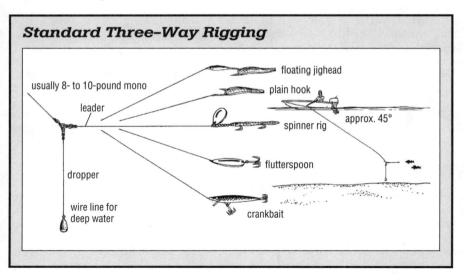

usually 8- to 10-pound mono

leader

floating jighead

plain hook

spinner rig

approx. 45°

dropper

flutterspoon

wire line for deep water

crankbait

Rig Advantages / Disadvantages

3-Way Rig	Advantages	Disadvantages
Presents livebait, floaters, spinners, crankbaits, and flutterspoons.	Precision depth control for fish suspended off bottom.	Tends to snag in brush.
	Able to drop rod tip back and give fish extra time to move with the bait.	Becomes unwieldy as dropper or leader exceeds 5 feet.
	Holds bait off bottom in current.	
	Good for both slow and quick presentations.	

Sinker—Depending on depth and boat speed, use a 3/8- to 3-ounce bell sinker beneath a dropper. Faster speeds and deeper water require heavier sinkers. Some anglers substitute the bell sinker with a heavy leadhead jig and soft plastic tail. The jig provides weight while adding an extra presentation element.

Connections—A three-way swivel holds this rig together, providing separate attachment points for main line, dropper, and leader. Sizes #2 to #8 suffice for most situations.

Leader—A 2- to 6-foot leader is standard. A shallow minnow plug trolled on a 4-foot dropper typically dives about 1 foot. A spinner rig and crawler behind a shorter leader have a greater tendency to trail directly behind the swivel, while longer leaders might cause the rig to sag toward bottom. Boat speed is also largely responsible for how certain lures respond. The rig should be fashioned to keep the lure traveling straight behind the swivel.

Knots—The three-way rig requires no fewer than five knots. Therefore, familiar, easy-to-tie terminal connectors like the Trilene knot are most useful.

Hooks—Variable, depending on lure or livebait rig.

Natural Baits—Nightcrawlers, leeches, and minnows remain standard livebait options. Catfish anglers using a three-way rig as a stationary or drift rig also employ cutbait, chicken livers, and other baits.

Artificial Baits—Similar to bottom-bouncer rigs, shallow-diving minnowbaits and light flutterspoons are commonly used for walleyes, trout, salmon, striped bass, pike, and muskies.

RIGGING WRINKLES

A number of interesting rigging variations lend additional utility to this already versatile presentation. The combinations are limited only by your imagination.

FISHING THE THREE-WAY RIG

Where & When—The three-way rig is an extremely versatile option for covering large expanses of clean-bottomed flats or structural edges. Most effective in water deeper than 15 feet, the rig excels where structure allows you to walk the sinker up and down slopes. By varying boat speed as well as dropper and leader length, you can manipulate how the rig works, including how far off bottom the bait runs. Three-way rigs typically target fish hovering within 6 feet of bottom.

Speed—From stationary against current in rivers (as your bait flutters behind the leader) to trolling speeds of perhaps 1/2 to 3 mph.

Presentation—Freespool the rig to the bottom using an appropriate sinker, usually 1 to 3 ounces. Engage the reel and begin moving forward with an outboard or electric motor. Adjust the amount of line beneath the boat depending on depth and boat speed. Ideally, you should feel the sinker frequently bump bottom, intermittently cutting through open water. You don't want to be continuously plowing a heavy ditch in the terrain because it will deaden your ability to detect strikes, and eventually snag weeds, rocks, or wood. Maintain a steep angle between your line and the water by retrieving or releasing line.

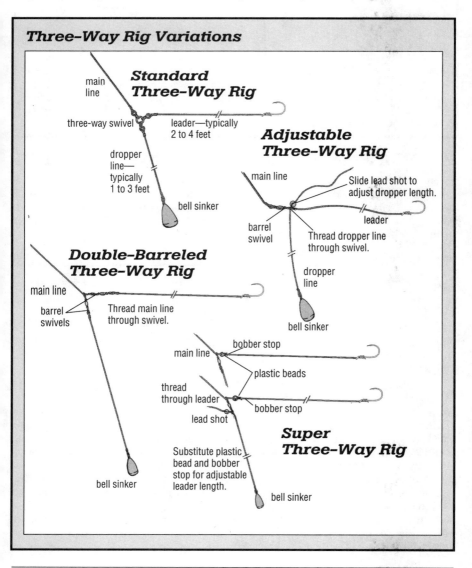

Three-Way Rig Variations

Standard Three-Way Rig

main line

three-way swivel

leader—typically 2 to 4 feet

dropper line— typically 1 to 3 feet

bell sinker

Adjustable Three-Way Rig

main line

Slide lead shot to adjust dropper length.

leader

barrel swivel

Thread dropper line through swivel.

dropper line

bell sinker

Double-Barreled Three-Way Rig

main line

barrel swivels

Thread main line through swivel.

bell sinker

Super Three-Way Rig

bobber stop

main line

plastic beads

thread through leader

bobber stop

lead shot

Substitute plastic bead and bobber stop for adjustable leader length.

bell sinker

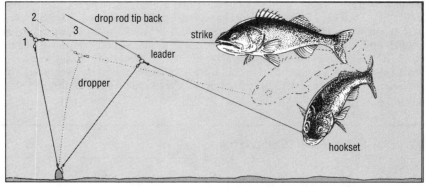

The Pivot Hookset

A 3-way rig allows you to drop the rod-tip back and give the fish extra time to move with the bait. (1) Strike. (2) Drop rod-tip back, grudgingly giving rod top to the fish. (3) When "V" between leader and dropper straightens, fish will be able to detect sinker. Set the hook.

PLANER BOARD & SNAP-ON SINKER RIGGING

Snap-on devices have brought the art of trolling to a new level. Put a lure behind the boat and start moving—you're trolling. Pinch on a sinker and your lure dives deeper. Clip a planer board to the line and your lures run farther away from the boat. In a matter of seconds, you've gone from one-dimensional to three-dimensional trolling, which will eventually make you three times more effective.

PRIMARY SPECIES

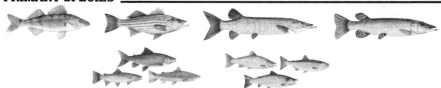

TACKLE

Rod & Reel—A 7½- to 8½-foot moderately-slow-action, medium-power casting or trolling rod; large-capacity casting reel, preferably with a built-in line counter.

Line—10- to 14-pound-test fused superlines match most trolling presentations. The low-stretch nature of these lines increases sensitivity. By feeling vibration you'll learn that each lure offers its own unique feel. Similarly, you know instantly, either by watching the rod tip or through touch, when a bait has fouled. This saves time and increases productivity because lures spend more time running properly.

Sinker—Numerous weighting options exist. Snap-on sinkers are the simplest weight system for trolling. Pinch the line clip, which holds various interchangeable sinker sizes, attaching it 10 to 50 feet ahead of the lure. Some anglers also pinch a single split shot ahead of the lure, not so much for extra depth, but to prevent floating weeds and other debris from fouling the plug.

Leadcore line essentially is a "built-in" sinker that carries a plug to a desired depth, based on trolling speed and length of line behind the boat. The typical setup involves a length of dacron backing spliced to 100 yards of 20- to 25-pound-test leadcore, which is simply lead line sheathed by dacron. The lure runs behind a 6- to 10-foot monofilament or fluorocarbon leader connected to the leadcore with a barrel swivel. In order to determine line length, leadcore is marked by a color change every 10 yards.

Connections—A small cross-lock-type snap enables quick, easy lure changes and allows a plug or spoon a wider range of movement. Other connections between line and a planer board or snap-on weight typically employ release clips, which grab and hold line.

Knots—Reliable terminal connections such as a Trilene knot work best. For tying directly to the plug, consider a loop knot, particularly if the plug lacks a split ring.

Hooks—Though the treble hooks on most plugs work fine, some fishermen replace them with premium trebles, which can hook and hold fish better. In all cases, periodically touch up points with a hook hone.

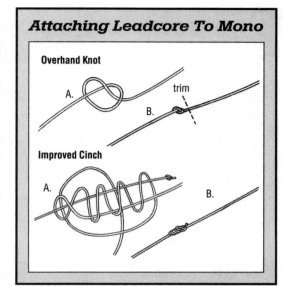

Attaching Leadcore To Mono

Overhand Knot

A.

B.

trim

Improved Cinch

A.

B.

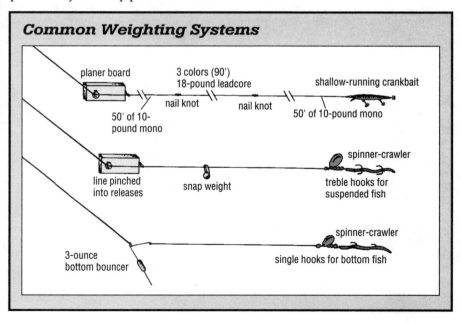

Common Weighting Systems

planer board

3 colors (90')
18-pound leadcore

shallow-running crankbait

nail knot

nail knot

50' of 10-
pound mono

50' of 10-pound mono

line pinched
into releases

snap weight

spinner-crawler

treble hooks for
suspended fish

3-ounce
bottom bouncer

spinner-crawler

single hooks for bottom fish

Drop And Dive

Whichever lure style you use, remember that it will generally dive or drop beneath a sinker, leadcore segment, or downrigger ball. Deep-diving crankbaits dive the most, shallow-running crankbaits less, then spinner rigs, and finally, thin flutterspoons. The longer the line, the more the drop, up to the point where water resistance causes it to begin rising. Thin flutterspoons on short leaders probably drop the least, running almost level behind the weight. Diving planers are generally run with short leaders, so lures dive or drop little.

When you set your lines, consider dive or drop. If a crankbait trolls 9 feet deep on 50 feet of 10-pound-test at 2 mph and you want to fish near the bottom, set your lines so the sinker rides about 10 or 12 feet above bottom. The lure's diving motion will take it within (theoretically) 1 or 2 feet of bottom, give or take a bit in big waves, on turns, or during variations in speed.

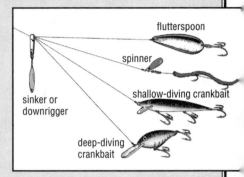

Planer Boards—Water pressure created by a moving boat and forced onto the board's flat surface planes it to the side. The more line that's released between the reel and the board, the farther from the boat the board runs. Planer boards spread lines away from the noise of a boat. They also allow multiple lures to be trolled away from each other, providing a larger coverage area. Let out a predetermined amount of line with a lure behind the boat—say, 100 to 200 feet. Engage the reel and fasten the board on the line with both clips.

Artificial Baits—Diving plugs, spoons, and other flashing lures, including spinner rigs and livebait combinations, take fish while trolling.

RIGGING WRINKLES

Beyond lure selection, trolling introduces a whole new set of variables calling for different tools. A properly rigged boat becomes part of the presentation. Tools such as strategically placed rod holders, digital speed indicators, and GPS mapping units—which track trolling passes in expanses of featureless water—work together to make trolling more effective.

PLANER BOARD TROLLING

Where & When—Anytime you need to cover a wide swath of water, particularly when fish spread out over open flats or suspend above deeper water, this trolling approach is deadly. Another situation for planer boards is trolling in shallow or clear water where fish continually spook away from baits trolled directly behind the boat. Planer boards deliver baits in water too shallow for boats to traverse.

Fishing High And Low

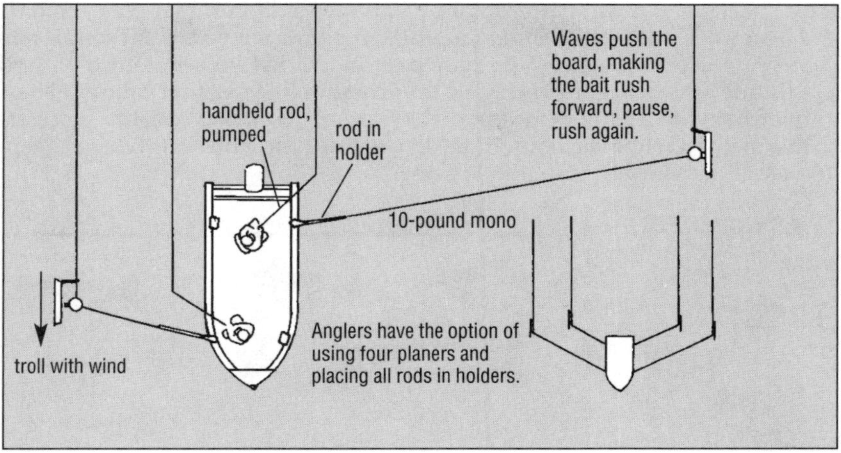

Waves push the board, making the bait rush forward, pause, rush again.

handheld rod, pumped

rod in holder

10-pound mono

troll with wind

Anglers have the option of using four planers and placing all rods in holders.

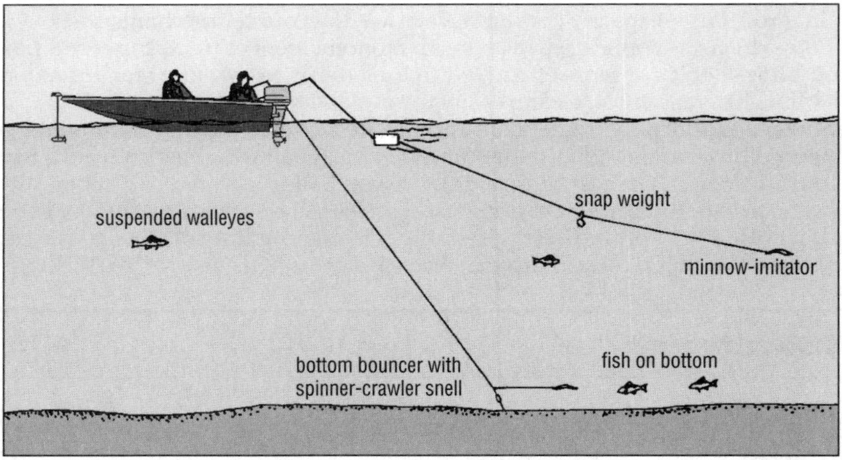

suspended walleyes

snap weight

minnow-imitator

bottom bouncer with spinner-crawler snell

fish on bottom

Speed—Usual trolling speeds range between 1 and 3 mph, though faster speeds have been known to work during the hottest periods of summer.

Presentation—Effective trolling means observing then duplicating each productive variable—lure depth, line length, speed, and successful trolling zones—then fine-tuning. Tools like a speed indicator, line-counter reel, and GPS ease the duplicating process. Of course, before even thinking about duplicating what's working, it's necessary to first understand the basic process of trolling. As a general rule, it's better to troll with, rather than against the wind.

DOWNRIGGING & OTHER DIVING DEVICES

This specialized trolling presentation employs a downrigger connected to a heavy lead weight to carry fishing line and bait into deep water. Although some anglers remain intimidated by the extra gear and added steps involved with rigging this trolling system, downrigging is fairly simple. Most first-time anglers, in fact, find that with a little instruction, they can rig, run, and become successful with this method within an hour. If you like to troll, particularly for fish in deeper water, learn this simple yet deadly rigging.

PRIMARY SPECIES

TACKLE

Rod & Reel—A 7- to 10-foot, slow- to moderate-action casting or fiberglass trolling rod; large-capacity casting reel with a line-counter mechanism.

Line—10- to 30-pound-test, low-stretch monofilament or fused superline. Low-stretch lines hook fish more effectively at long distances, while a small-diameter line offers less resistance, slicing easily through deep water.

Sinker—Heavy downrigger balls carry trolled lures to extreme depths and are measured by pounds rather than ounces. Typical ball weights run from 4 to 10 pounds or more. While trolling, a downrigger ball is lowered to a set depth—based on fish location and lure running depth—attached to the downrigger boom, via a length of 150-pound-test wire cable. The fishing line attaches to the cannonball with a quick-release clip that frees the line when a fish strikes the bait.

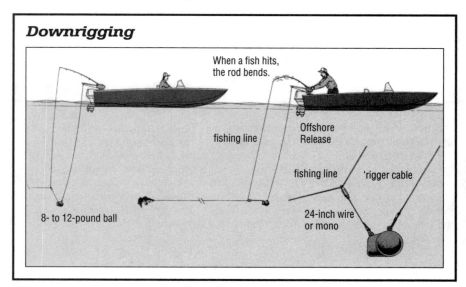

Downrigging

When a fish hits, the rod bends.

fishing line

Offshore Release

fishing line   'rigger cable

8- to 12-pound ball

24-inch wire or mono

Weights And Diving Devices

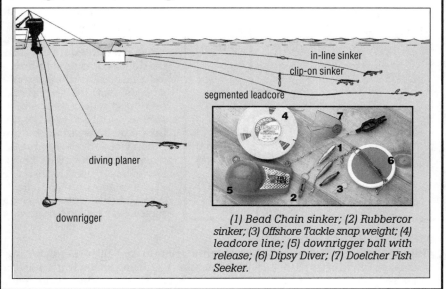

in-line sinker

clip-on sinker

segmented leadcore

diving planer

downrigger

(1) Bead Chain sinker; (2) Rubbercor sinker; (3) Offshore Tackle snap weight; (4) leadcore line; (5) downrigger ball with release; (6) Dipsy Diver; (7) Doelcher Fish Seeker.

Connections—A Cross-Lok snap tied to the end of the main line facilitates lure changes. Other terminal connections relate directly to the downrigger cable and ball. These connections are made with downrigger components such as a quick release and a stacker. Downrigger terminal kits include most of these components.

Knots—Unless you're using additional trolling devices, such as a Dipsy Diver or a dodger, or running a leader to the lure, the most important knot is the one that connects line to lure. A Trilene knot is a good choice.

Downrigger—This simple device consists of a wheel that holds approximately 150 feet of steel cable, which can be released or retracted with a manual or motorized crank. Most downriggers contain a 3-digit depth counter, displaying how deep the ball has descended. Cable runs from the wheel to a boom arm, which projects from the base of the unit at roughly a 45-degree angle then swivels around a small pulley, which helps regulate cable release. Also projecting from the unit's base are a ball holder and a tubular rod holder, sloped slightly steeper than the angle of the boom.

Artificial Baits—Common lures include diving minnowbaits, J-plugs, spoons, and flash rigs such as cowbells or a series of spinners ahead of a hook. In addition, West Coast and Great Lakes salmon and lake trout anglers often use dodgers to attract suspended fish from long range. Dodgers, also called flashers, consist of a 4- to 11-inch oval-shaped plate, usually beveled at each end to produce fish-attracting sound and action. These brightly colored devices sport a swivel at each end so they can be rigged in-line, roughly 8 to 36 inches ahead of a light spoon, tinsel fly, or plastic squid. When trolled, dodgers swing back and forth erratically, imparting enticing actions to trailing lures or deadbaits—a lethal presentation for salmon.

Natural Baits—While not a common practice, some anglers troll livebaits, particularly large minnows, for striped bass and muskies in deep water. Walleye anglers also troll spinner rigs with nightcrawlers behind downriggers.

Angle Of Attack

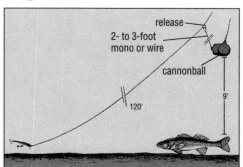

The lure dives 8 feet on 120 feet of 10-pound-test. With the ball 9 feet off the bottom, the lure runs about 1 foot from bottom.

RIGGING WRINKLES

To achieve vertical control of lure depth and a horizontal spread to the side of the boat, many anglers use a Dipsy Diver. This disc-shaped device, like the dodger, is rigged in-line, 6 to 10 feet ahead of a lure. Because it pulls so hard, the Diver should be rigged with a 6- to 8-inch rubber snubber ahead of the lure, which keeps hooks from pulling loose or the line breaking when a fish strikes. Dipsy Divers and other stand-alone diving planers also pull lures down into the depths, so downriggers aren't always necessary.

DOWNRIGGER TROLLING

Where & When—Downrigging offers the ultimate in controlled-depth fishing. Say you spot intermittent fish marks on sonar while cruising above water 100 feet deep, most lying 58 feet down. By watching the depth counter as the ball descends and calculating lure diving depth, you can fish precisely at the 57- to 58-foot range—exactly where your lure needs to be to catch fish.

Speed—Trolling speeds of 1 to 3 mph are common, though salmon anglers often troll much faster.

Presentation—The mechanics of downrigger trolling differ slightly from basic trolling. Learn how the downrigger works together with the wire cable, cannonball, quick release, and rod, including what happens when a fish hits. Perhaps the most important detail is discerning how different fish trip the quick-release mechanism, which usually can be adjusted from tight to loose.

Zeroing In With Downriggers

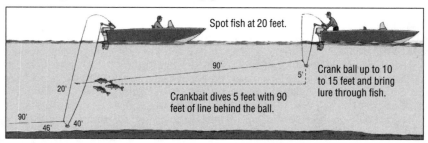

With leadcore or Dipsys, exact depth is a guess. You eventually zero in on fish through success with a certain setup, duplicating it on other lines.

Downriggers, however, allow precise depth control. You put your lure at the exact depth of the fish and can react to fish elsewhere in the water column the instant you see them on your electronics. Only trolling with wire line may be more exacting.

Chapter 4

Float Rigs

FLOAT APPLICATIONS A TO Z

Modern float fishing has evolved greatly since the days of red-and-white bobbers. We now enjoy widespread success with float & livebait systems, even in deep water.

Today's floats are available in many forms and are fashioned from various materials—from classic corks to hollow plastic bobbers that clip to the line, to balsa floats that slide on the line. Many are perfectly balanced to match a specific weight. The ideal float remains just barely buoyant while supporting a sinker and bait. When a fish takes, it feels little resistance, easily pulling the float beneath the surface.

Beyond buoyancy, float designers consider the effects of current and wind on some models. The right float should not be blown out of position by wind or whisked away by current, but rather should drift naturally at about current speed. Modern float rigs are an efficient and refined presentation method for virtually any fish species.

Floats!

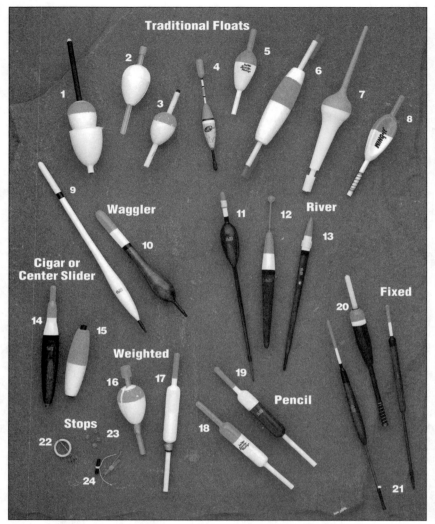

Traditional Floats

Waggler

River

Cigar or Center Slider

Fixed

Weighted

Pencil

Stops

Traditional: *(1) Oxboro Bob-A-Jig; (2) Freshwater Tackle Easy On; (3) HiFloat Glo; (4) Gapen Slip-N-Lock; (5) Stinger Tackle SK4-000 Leech; (6) R N B Tackle Slip N Set; (7) Tackle 2000 Rocket Bobber; (8) Carlson Wing-It (fixed or slip).* **Waggler:** *(9) Thill Stealth; (10) Thill Bodied Waggler.* **River:** *(11) Thill River Master (fixed); (12) Thill Double Ring Slider; (13) Thill Smooth Stream (fixed).* **Cigar or Center Slider:** *(14) Thill Mille Lacs Special; (15) Oxboro Bob-A-Jig.* **Weighted:** *(16) Freshwater Tackle Easy On; (17) Thill Weighted Float.* **Pencil:** *(18) Stinger Tackle SK5-000 Light-Bite; (19) Thill American Classic Pencil.* **Fixed:** *(20) Thill Shy Bite with and without Thill Float Swivel Adapter (converts to a slipfloat); (21) Wazp Night Rider S-NR586.* **Stops:** *(22) neoprene; (23) plastic beads; (24) string.*

Some of the first floats available in North America featured a retractable wire clip that pinched the line, holding the float in place. Most of us have seen or used red and white ball-shaped bobbers at one time or another. They remain a reliable, easy-to-rig option for drifting or suspending baits above the bottom, particularly in shallow water.

PRIMARY SPECIES

TACKLE

Rod & Reel—A 6½- to 8-foot, slow- to moderate-action, light- to medium-power spinning rod; medium-capacity spinning reel with a long-cast spool. This combo allows for long lob casts and sweeping hooksets.

Line—4- to 8-pound-test monofilament.

Floats—Fixed floats attach to a set point on the line using a variety of mechanisms. Thin quill-type floats use a piece of silicone tubing to secure the line to the float stem. A spring-lock float contains a notch at the bottom of the stem where line passes through. The spring is released over the line, locking the float in place. Another simple fixed float is made from a balloon. Anglers of striped bass, large-mouth bass, and catfish often use balloon floats to suspend large, lively baitfish. Inflate the balloon to roughly the size of a plum, tie an overhand knot over the line, and slide it to the desired depth.

Other models have holes drilled through their length. Line is passed through the hole from top to bottom, and a peg is inserted into the top of the float to secure it in place on the line. Similarly, the ever-popular clip-on bobber sports retractable line clips on both ends of its ball-shaped body.

Finally, casting bubbles are designed to be filled with water to add weight for longer casts. Bubbles typically are made from translucent plastic and feature a rubber line guide that twists to lock the float in position.

Sinker—Most anglers employ one to several small split shots or a larger pinch-on sinker between float and bait. When using a leadhead jig instead of a hook, extra weight may not be necessary.

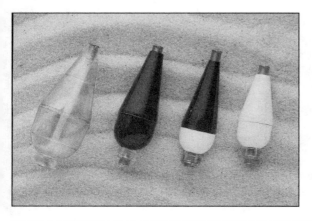

Filled with a little water, the Rainbow Plastics A-Just-A-Bubble casts easily and then sits unobtrusively at the surface of the water. When a crappie or other panfish takes it, the water instantly settles to the thick end of the float, allowing the pointed end to tip up without resistance. Set the hook. Don't wait for fish to pull the float down.

Working The 'Bubble

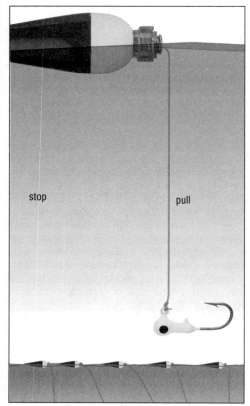

stop   pull

Work the Rainbow Plastics A-Just-A-Bubble by pulling it forward a foot to allow the jig to settle back below the float. Fish take as the jig settles or rides stationary below the bubble.

Connections—Typically unnecessary, though some anglers prefer to add a swivel between the float and sinker to reduce line twist and facilitate rig changes.

Knots—Standard knots such as the Trilene work fine.

Hooks—Plain hooks and jigheads can be used to present livebait beneath a fixed float. When choosing between the two, it's helpful to realize that a jighead adds a bit of attracting color and anchors a livebait in place, while a plain hook allows a minnow or leech to swim in a wider arc around the float.

For baits like minnows, leeches, and crickets, #8 to #2 Aberdeen-style hooks work best. Hook minnows just beneath the dorsal fin, parallel to their body, with the hook point toward the head. For angleworms and nightcrawlers, use a #8 to #4 baitholder hook. When fish continually steal portions of your worm, try bunching it on a hook, threading it well onto the shank, leaving only a small tail for fish to nip.

Natural Baits—Worms, leeches, minnows, crickets, grasshoppers, hellgrammites, and insect larva all take fish beneath a fixed float. Whole or cut portions of baitfish also work well with fixed floats, particularly for catfish and pike.

Artificial Baits—When fish such as small bass, sunfish, or perch are feeding aggressively, it might be preferable to substitute a small plastic bait or hair jig for livebait. Anglers using a casting bubble for trout feeding on or near the surface often use a small dry or wet fly.

FISHING A FIXED FLOAT

Where & When—Fixed floats teamed with bait work best in water less than about 4 feet deep. Deeper water makes casting difficult because of the length of the rig. Such water calls for a slipfloat rig. Fixed float situations include fish feeding just above shallow snags, or on or near the surface, perhaps over moderately deep water.

Presentation—The best presentation with a bobber often is no retrieve at all—simply cast to a good spot and let the rig sit, or allow a gentle breeze to slowly drift it along. That's why active livebait can be important. Let the bait do most of the fish-attracting work.

In other cases, though, you might need to give the bait a bit of action to trigger fish. Small twitches with the rod tip impart up and down bobs to the float, jiggling the bait in an enticing manner. Or give the rod a quick sweep toward you, immediately reeling in slack line as the bait darts forward, then settles back down. Always follow any retrieve with a pause of at least several seconds.

SLIPFLOAT RIGS

The beauty of slipfloats is that they slide up and down the line to facilitate fishing near bottom in water deeper than the length of the rod. When a slipfloat hits the water, weight below carries line through a hole in the body of the float until it meets a stop knot—sort of a retractable fishing rig.

PRIMARY SPECIES

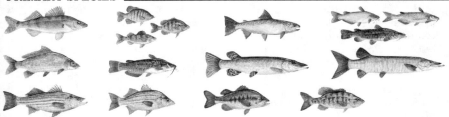

TACKLE

Rod & Reel—A 7- to 12-foot, slow- to moderate-action, medium-power spinning rod; medium-capacity spinning reel with a long-cast spool. Rods with a soft tip section allow for longer casts with soft baits, while increased rod length allows for better hooksets, especially at long range.

Line—4- to 8-pound-test monofilament. For larger fish such as pike, muskies, stripers, or catfish, consider using 10- to 20-pound monofilament or heavier superlines.

Floats—So many slipfloat styles exist that it's helpful to classify designs into categories. Carlisle-style floats remain the most commonly used design. They're a fine, general-use float, moderately buoyant and moderately stable in current. Cigar floats sport a slightly bulkier profile requiring greater force to pull them under. Bulbous floats offer more stability in current, but they're also more easily blown around in wind. Consider using a cigar float with larger baitfish.

On extreme ends of the scale, gazette floats are the widest, most buoyant designs, while super-streamlined pencil and waggler-style floats sink with little resistance.

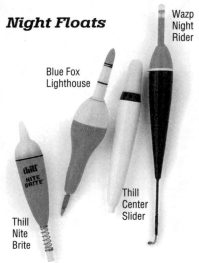

Night Floats

Wazp Night Rider

Blue Fox Lighthouse

Thill Center Slider

Thill Nite Brite

Slipfloat Shapes

Classic slipfloats have a line-through-stem design for quick, efficient passage of line. Pencil-style slipfloats (Thill), one of the five basic float groups, offer advantages in some conditions. The slimmer profile is less obtrusive in shallow water over spooky fish (especially in natural wood tones). This shape slides under quicker on the strike, offering less resistance to the fish.

The Carlson Wing-It has a compromise shape. The clefts carved into the body of the float (creating the wings) allow this float to slip under almost as efficiently as the pencil style, yet it casts better. It retains many qualities of the more buoyant, classic round-body floats.

Standard slipfloats with a short, squat shape (Thill) ride waves better, are easier to control in wind, and ride at a reasonable pace in higher winds. Tall standard slipfloats (Strictly Walleye) catch more wind and move at a more acceptable pace in a breeze for covering flats or the tops of reefs.

Balanced weighted versions of any design (Thill) should require no weight on the line for a slower, more-enticing drop speed. The Thill Center Slider is the most stable design when weighted properly. For optimum balance in buoyancy on most floats, the waterline should mimic the line separating two colors on the float's body, as on the Center Slider. This is a good design for actively jigging with bait, plastics, or blade baits.

The Thill Minnow-Ring Slider is a good tool for drifting active baits like minnows across flats in a breeze. This design differs from the classics. Line moving through two rings outside the float passes less efficiently, making it a poor choice with jigging lures but more versatile to rig.

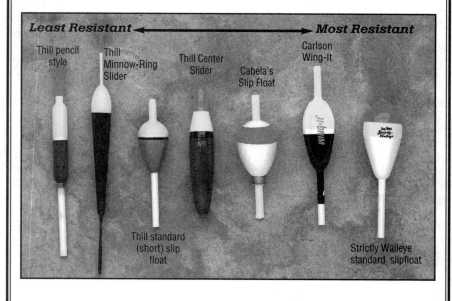

Least Resistant → Most Resistant

Thill pencil style

Thill Minnow-Ring Slider

Thill Center Slider

Cabela's Slip Float

Carlson Wing-It

Thill standard (short) slip float

Strictly Walleye standard slipfloat

Tying Your Own Stop Knots

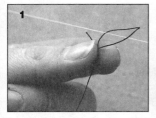

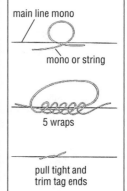
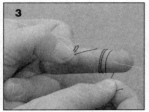

1

2

3

4

main line mono

mono or string

5 wraps

pull tight and
trim tag ends

To tie your own float stops, tie a nail knot over your main line with a piece of monofilament or string. (1) Make a loop in the knot and pinch it. (2) Wrap the string 5 times around the line and the tip of your middle finger. (3) Run the end of the string through the five loops and the original loop. Grab both ends and cinch it tight. Use a bead as a buffer between the float and the stop.

In addition, a number of hybrid float designs offer even greater flexibility. Many European-style floats excel for shore fishing. Finally, for night fishing, several companies offer lighted floats, the most useful incorporating small lithium batteries that plug into an internal light bulb on the tip of the float.

Sinker—Use one to several split shots or a single pinch-on sinker between float and bait. When using a leadhead jig instead of a hook, extra weight might not be necessary.

Connections—Unnecessary, though some anglers prefer to add a swivel between float and sinker to reduce line twist and facilitate leader changes.

Knots—A Trilene knot works fine for attaching terminal components. A specialized stop knot tied with a short length of Dacron line allows for adjusting depth by sliding the stop knot up and down the main line above the float. Many anglers purchase packages of pretied stop knots, but it's easy to learn this simple knot. Commercial stop knots come affixed to a short piece of plastic tubing. The main line runs through the tube and the knot slides off onto the line and then is tightened into place. Most anglers position a small plastic bead between the stop knot and the float to serve as a buffer, preventing the knot from wedging into the float stem.

Hooks—Plain hooks and jigheads can be used to present livebait beneath a slipfloat. When choosing between the two, it's helpful to realize that a jighead adds a bit of attracting color and serves to anchor a livebait in place, while a plain hook allows a minnow or leech to swim in a wider arc around the float.

When using leeches, a #10 to #6 light-wire Aberdeen hook works well, while worms and crawlers call for a #8 to #4 baitholder. For small to medium-sized minnows, go with a #6 to #1 Aberdeen or wide-gap hook. Larger baitfish require even larger wide-gap hooks, up to 8/0 for flathead catfish or muskies.

Hooks & Components

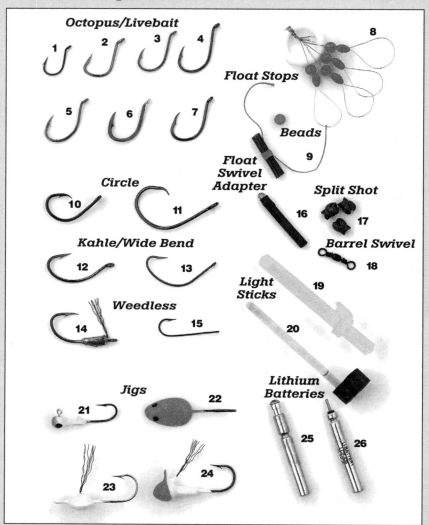

Octopus/Livebait
1 2 3 4
5 6 7

Float Stops 8

Beads

Circle 10 11

Float Swivel Adapter 9

Split Shot 16 17

Kahle/Wide Bend 12 13

Barrel Swivel 18

Weedless 14 15

Light Sticks 19 20

Jigs 21 22 23 24

Lithium Batteries 25 26

Octopus/Livebait: *(1) Berkley Gold Point LBH; (2) Mustad Ultra Grip Bait 38971; (3) Daiichi Bait Hook Wide Gap D162; (4) Gamakatsu 02508; (5) VMC Ultimate Octopus V7199RD; (6) Eagle Claw L195; (7) Owner SSW 5111-071.* **Float Stops:** *(8) Wazp (neoprene); (9) Hook'um (string).* **Circle:** *(10) Eagle Claw Featherlite L702G; (11) Eagle Claw Featherlite L787G.* **Kahle/Wide Bend:** *(12) VMC Wide Gap Walleye 7105BN; (13) Eagle Claw L741G.* **Weedless:** *(14) Stinger Weedless; (15) Tru-Turn Fine Wire 860ZS.* **Float Swivel Adapter:** *(16) Thill.* **Split Shot:** *(17) Bullet Weights #BB.* **Barrel Swivel:** *(18) #12 South Bend.* **Light Sticks:** *(19) Thill Night Light Float Kit; (20) Rod-N-Bobb Beacon.* **Jigs:** *(21) Northland Jig Head; (22) Freshwater Tackle Angle Jig; (23) Stinger Deluxe Timber Jig; (24) Stinger Timber Jig.* **Lithium Batteries:** *(25) Thill; (26) Blue Fox.*

Many hook makers offer colored hooks, which can help focus a fish's attention on the bait. Circle hooks also work with floats and reduce instances of throat-hooked fish.

Top jighead options include light heads, 1/32 to 1/8 ounce, and #2 or #4 hooks. Most jigs work under a float. The key is to properly match the jig or hook to the bait to cover conditions. When fishing in weeds or wood, for example, choose jigs with light-wire weedguards.

Natural Baits—When chasing walleyes and smallmouth bass, leeches remain the most popular livebait, undulating so enticingly that even the most discerning fish can't resist them. Just as effective in many situations and for many fish species, minnows and nightcrawlers also produce under a float. Large predators such as muskies, striped bass, largemouth bass, catfish, and big trout often go for a super-sized baitfish. When pursuing panfish, small insect larva, including waxworms and maggots, prove particularly effective.

Fine Points Of Float Fishing

Euro Rigging

Bobber tends to plunge in large waves.

bobber stop

bead

lead shot spaced to flutter hook and bait toward bottom

18"

Standard Rigging

wind

optional plastic bead

bobber stop

bulk shot pattern to plunge rig toward bottom

18"

Hook rises and twitches during a fast drift in waves.

Jig Rigging

optional intermediate split shot if necessary

Weight of jighead maintains vertical position on-off or near bottom.

Jig snaps up and down in waves.

Slipbobber hooks should penetrate with little pressure on light line. Light-wire Aberdeen styles are ideal, as are wide-bend Kahles, which contain a bit more steel but have excellent biting and holding characteristics. Octopus-style hooks, standard for livebait rigging, are excellent too, in bronze or black for low visibility in clear water; gold, red, blue, yellow, or silver to add color in dingy water. Weedless hooks help deflect snags in weeds and wood.

Jigheads in the 1/32-, 1/16-, and 1/8-ounce categories cover the bases for slipfloat walleyes. Round heads move up-down; planing heads flutter and swim. Try bright fluorescent yellow, chartreuse, or orange in dark or muddy water or in windy conditions. In clear water, black or plain lead may excel. At night, phosphorescent jigs may be the hot ticket.

Hook leeches just behind the sucker, which allows them to swim actively. Minnows should be hooked parallel to the dorsal fin. Hook crawlers once through the head or tail.

Other natural baits, particularly dead baitfish, produce plenty of fish such as channel and blue catfish and northern pike. Cutbait works best for cats, while pike usually prefer whole deadbaits. Finally, for bottom feeders such as carp, kernels of sweet corn can't be beat.

RIGGING WRINKLES

Beyond experimenting with different float, jighead, hook, and bait combinations, perhaps the most intriguing wrinkles are European modifications (see Chapter 6). The float paternoster rig, for example, prevents the float and bait from drifting when a bell sinker is placed at the base of the rig, while the livebait swims above, tethered to a dropper.

FISHING THE SLIPFLOAT RIG

Where & When—Floats are particularly effective for approaching fish swimming over shallow rocks, weedbeds, and clean flats, but they also work well in deeper water when a slow, deliberate presentation is necessary. Quietly drifting the right float and bait into position will eventually trigger a strike.

Presentation—Most float-fishing scenarios call for fishing either from shore or from an anchored boat. Position near the target area, preferably upwind or upcurrent, and lob the rig into position. If you're not well acquainted with the area, mark the key spot with a small buoy. Anchor within easy casting-distance and begin fishing.

Using a long, soft-tipped spinning rod, gently swing the rig sideways and behind you, then thrust the rod toward the target in a slight upward motion as you release line. Think of the cast as a soft lob, like tossing an underhand pitch. Remember, you're trying to hit your target with as little impact as possible.

Use the wind to your advantage, rather than fighting it. Cast a short distance and allow the wind to carry the rig into the target zone. From a downwind position, cast the rig beyond the target, allowing the wind to drift the float through the fish.

Jigs & Jigging

A MOST PRECISE & VERSATILE APPROACH

A jig is a rig and a rig is a jig. It is in understanding how one is the other that you can improve your fishing. The central idea in rigging and jigging is to keep a livebait where you want it, usually near bottom. Fish love livebait, although when they're feeding aggressively, they can often be fooled into thinking an imitation is the real thing. In this sense, then, a bare-bones jig tipped with something like a golden shiner is properly classified as a rig, whereas a jig dressed with a plastic tail is a lure.

JIG AND BAIT RIGGING

Because of their wide-reaching versatility, jigs can catch aggressive, neutral, and even tentative fish of almost any species. This flexibility elevates the simple leadhead jig to the closest thing to a magic lure.

Jig Features

(A) Head Design—Important aspects are shape and weight. Shapes can knife through current (bullet heads), tip a minnow head-down and tail-up (stand-up), swim over snaggy bottoms, slow drop-speed in shallow cover, balance vertically, and several other options. Weight is matched to conditions like wind and current or entirely to depth. Depth and speed control are the most important considerations when choosing a head design.

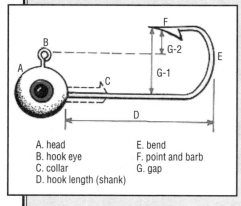

A. head
B. hook eye
C. collar
D. hook length (shank)
E. bend
F. point and barb
G. gap

(B) Placement of the hook eye affects how a jig falls, how it lifts off bottom, and how the package moves or swims—An eye slightly back of center balances a bait in a horizontal position better for vertical jigging, and an eye slightly forward of center allows you to lift a jig cleanly off bottom with less force when casting.

(C) Hook construction—Use thin, fine-wire hooks with a wide bend for light line; thicker steel for heavy line. Check hooks before buying to see how easily they bend. Some jigs still offer less than premium hooks.

(D) Hook length or shank affects size and action of the package—Short hooks are preferred early in the season; less of a mouthful, less bait action. Long hooks "swim" better, produce a longer profile, and secure nightcrawlers best. Longer, lighter hooks "pivot" toward fish trying to inhale the bait, so they tend to hook better for vertical jigging. Short, compact packages rise and fall quickly on lift-fall retrieves; fish are more likely to engulf the entire package.

(E) Originally jigs had no collars— Mister Twister developed collars in the early 1970s for securing plastic bodies. Collars are now a standard feature. Three-barb and four-barb variations excel for securing live nightcrawlers.

(F) The hook point should be short and the barb small—Reduce big barbs with a file. Points should be razor sharp and checked regularly after fishing near rocks and wood. Improved hook designs include harder alloys that dull less frequently. Straight points (as shown) are often preferred to beak hooks (curved points) because penetration is believed to be quicker.

(G) Old jig designs had narrow hook gaps—Gaps opened over the years because big gaps (G-1) hook better. Jaw bones and plates must fit between the hook point and the jighead (G-2), which is the true measurement of gap on a jighead. Gaps should be opened slightly on today's average jig, but not if the hook is too light and has a tendency to straighten.

Jigs lend a large degree of hands-on control to presenting a bait. In other words, an angler casting and retrieving a jig-minnow combination possesses a direct connection to what the bait is doing. When you twitch the rod tip, the minnow immediately bounces and jiggles along behind the jighead. At rest, the minnow is trapped against the jighead, able only to struggle against the weight of the anchor. The jighead is this anchor, one that's close to the bait—hence, more control. In this sense, a jig is a rig.

PRIMARY SPECIES

TACKLE

Rod & Reel—5½- to 7-foot, moderate- to moderately-fast action, light- to medium-power spinning rod with a soft tip; medium-capacity spinning reel.

Line—6- to 10-pound, low-stretch monofilament.

Sinker—The lead portion of the jig comprises the sinker. Shape, size (weight), and color vary to extremes. Familiar head shapes include ball, bullet, mushroom, darter, stand-up, swimming, and many others.

Jig Design And Function

Head Design	Example	Original Intended Use
Tear (bullet)		original swimming design
Round		original vertical jigging design
Keel		vertical use in current
Swimming		swimming through weeds, originally a design for bass

First, get comfortable using standard ball-shaped heads, which is what most anglers use most often. Later, you might want to try stand-up heads for snaggy bottoms or wedge-shaped heads for fishing through weeds. Then, experiment with other shapes.

Knots—Improved clinch, Trilene, or palomar knots make solid line-to-jig connections. Occasionally, to achieve a freer range of movements, tie a loop knot, such as a Duncan loop, to the jig.

Hook—Shank length and gap remain the two major design variables. "Tipping jigs," those designed for use with natural baits, commonly model both a short-shank hook and a wide gap to accommodate larger livebaits like minnows, while still leaving enough bite to hook fish. Always keep hook points needle sharp by touching them up with a hook hone.

Natural Baits—When casting and retrieving or trolling a jig and minnow, hook a baitfish under the lower jaw and out through the upper jaw. Many anglers prefer to insert the jig hook into the minnow's mouth and out behind the head to prevent flinging the minnow off the jig.

As an effective alternative to lip hooking, "reverse rigging" allows a jig to be fished slowly, often stationary, directly below a boat or under a float. Pierce the minnow's skin just behind the dorsal fin, then turn and run the hook lightly along its back and out. By hooking the baitfish parallel to the dorsal fin, the jig lies in perfect position to hook fish that commonly eat other fish headfirst.

Hooking other baits, such as leeches, is almost always dictated by a need to present the jig and bait in a natural, streamlined manner. Insert the hook into a ribbon leech just behind the middle of the large sucker (tail end) and out.

With a nightcrawler, pop the hook into the top of the head (dark end) and thread the worm straight onto the jig the length of the hook shank. This method is particularly effective on jigs with barbed collars designed to hold soft plastic baits. If you're using a jig with a shorter shank, run the hook one time through the crawler's head. Another especially effective method when dealing with short-striking walleyes

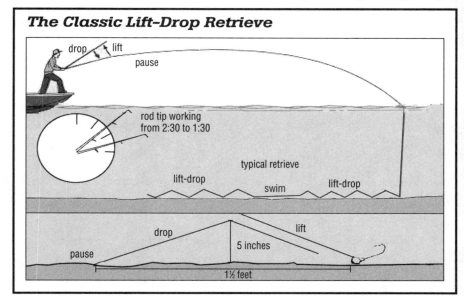

The Classic Lift-Drop Retrieve

drop — lift
pause

rod tip working
from 2:30 to 1:30

typical retrieve

lift-drop
swim
lift-drop

drop
lift
5 inches
pause
1½ feet

is called "skewering." Break the crawler in half, insert the hook into the open body cavity of a half crawler, and thread it up the hook shank and onto the barb. This forces fish to bite much closer to the jighead, where they're usually hooked.

Less common baits, such as crayfish, work best when hooked once through the back of the tail, underside and out. Finally, anglers using leopard frogs and waterdogs prefer the jaw-hooking method.

Stinger Hooks

RIGGING WRINKLES

Various artificial body dressings can be added, which produce different profiles and actions to jig and bait presentations. For instance, by adding a soft plastic grub—twistertail, split tail, shad tail—the jig glides a bit more and sinks slower during the retrieve. Similarly, some jigs sprout synthetic or artificial tails of hair. Marabou, bucktail, and synthetics produce similar, yet slightly different effects to jig-and-bait combos—again, slowing jig descent and adding color. Hair fibers quiver and "breath" underwater, even at rest, which often triggers fish to strike. Other refinements to jig design include small propellers and flicker spinners, which slightly alter action and vibration.

When dealing with short-striking fish, many anglers add a stinger hook. The stinger trails behind the jig where it's secured into the back portion of the bait. Most stingers are fashioned from a #8 or #6 treble hook fastened to a 2- to 3-inch piece of monofilament attached to a jig eye or hook.

Finally, many anglers add a small rattle chamber to the hook shank, which might attract more fish in some situations.

FISHING A JIG AND BAIT COMBO

Where & When—So many appropriate jig-fishing situations exist that it's difficult to describe specific situations. Jigs excel when targeting schools of fish holding near structure or cover, particularly fish lying close to the bottom. Retrieved at medium to fast speeds, jigs work as search lures when cast from shore or from a boat. But jigs also appeal to fish requiring a much slower retrieve speed.

Presentation—Jigs can be cast and retrieved or fished vertically beneath a float or through the ice. They work when fished stationary on bottom or slowly drifted with current. Perhaps the only wrong way to fish a jig is to move it too fast. Keeping a jig near bottom, while alternatively twitching and pausing it, rarely fails to produce. Sweep the rod tip forward a few inches to dance the jig off bottom. This is an attracting maneuver. Then, maintaining a taut line, pause the retrieve as the jig settles and rests back on bottom, which usually triggers fish to strike. Try to visualize in your mind exactly what that jig and bait look like, darting off bottom, then sinking back down. Experiment with different actions—from gradual swimming motions to erratic hops, interspersed with pauses, to let the bait settle and work in place.

JIG AND ARTIFICIAL BAIT RIGGING

I pressed to choose a single lure for any fish that swims, many of America's best anglers would select a jig and some type of soft plastic tail. Stemming back to the late 1960s and early 1970s, soft plastic lures like the Vibrotail, Method Reaper, Tweetle Bug, Puddle Jumper, and Mister Twister gradually found their way onto the rods of many anglers. On this front, today's big news includes increasingly lifelike baits impregnated with various scent and flavor enhancements. Many manufacturers now produce species-specific jigs—bass jigs, walleye jigs, panfish jigs, trout jigs, muskie jigs, even catfish jigs. Every year, too, these lures get a little better: they become a little more in tune with the preferences of each species.

Yet, while no two jigs look or act completely alike, each relies principally on a basic concept—a head-weighted hook and a leadhead jig, to deliver the goods in a manner attractive to fish.

PRIMARY SPECIES

TACKLE

Rod & Reel—Depends on cover conditions as well as fish size and species. Use a 6- to 7-foot, moderately-fast to fast-action, medium-power spinning rod coupled with a medium-capacity spinning reel and a long-cast spool. For heavy cover, a 7½-foot, moderately fast-action, heavy-power flipping stick teamed with a medium-capacity casting reel works well.

Line—4- to 10-pound-test, low-stretch monofilament line. Use the heaviest line you can get away with while maintaining depth and swimming action. When fishing weedless jigs for bass in heavy cover, heavier lines are a better choice.

Sinker—The weight of the jighead serves as the sinker. The shape of the head determines action, fall rate, weedlessness, and other factors. Common head shapes include ball, bullet, mushroom, darter, stand-up, swimming, and many others.

Knots—Improved clinch, Trilene, or palomar knots make solid line-to-jig connections. To achieve a freer range of movement, some anglers attach jigs with a loop knot.

Hook—Shank length and hook gap are the two major design variables. Jigs intended for soft plastic bodies often sport a barbed collar, which secures plastic and offers a slightly longer shank than jigs designed for use with livebait. Align soft plastic baits to run

Jigs For Fishing Plastic Baits

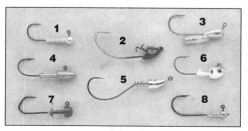

(1) Lunker City Lunker Grip; (2) Legacy-Lock; (3) K & E Rattling Tube Jig Head; (4) Owner Darter Head; (5) Legacy-Lock; (6) Matzuo Heavy Metal Jighead; (7) Gopher Mushroom Head; (8) Yamamoto Ballhead.

Matching Plastic Bodies To Fish Activity And Aggressiveness

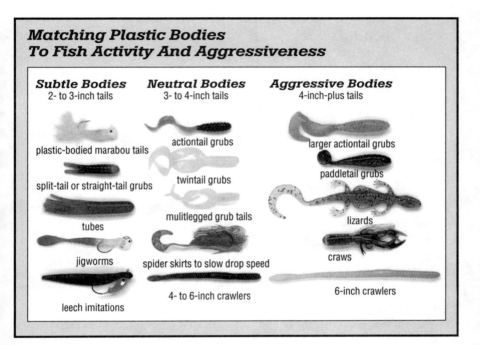

Subtle Bodies
2- to 3-inch tails

plastic-bodied marabou tails

split-tail or straight-tail grubs

tubes

jigworms

leech imitations

Neutral Bodies
3- to 4-inch tails

actiontail grubs

twintail grubs

mulitlegged grub tails

spider skirts to slow drop speed

4- to 6-inch crawlers

Aggressive Bodies
4-inch-plus tails

larger actiontail grubs

paddletail grubs

lizards

craws

6-inch crawlers

straight. Insert the hook into the tip of the bait's nose. Being careful to keep the hook in the middle of the plastic body, push the bait up the length of the hook shank, threading it straight onto the collar. Measure the distance of the hook shank against the plastic body; that's where you'll want to expose the point of the hook. Threaded correctly, the bait will hang perfectly straight.

Soft Plastics—Where anglers once had only two or three soft plastic body shapes to choose from, dozens of options exist today. Shads, twisters, tubes, split tails, lizards, reapers, paddletails, straight tails, leeches, and swimming minnows all work with jigs. Don't let the choices confuse you. Get comfortable with a few classics—a shad and a twister, for example. In fact, if you never fish anything but these two styles, you'll catch fish.

Other Artificial Jig Dressings—Many jig styles sprout different forms of hair, tentacle, or leg-like fibers. Materials such as colored living rubber and silicone commonly adorn jigs designed for largemouth bass, which usually include a strong plastic fiber weedguard for fishing thick cover. Many panfish and smallmouth bass jigs are dressed with natural hair fibers, including deer (bucktail), marabou, rabbit, and chicken feathers. In addition, synthetic fibers add attracting color and bulk to jigs.

RIGGING WRINKLES

Beyond head shape, color, and body material, some jigs contain extras such as an internal rattle chamber or an attached spinner or propeller to attract more fish. Some panfish anglers add clip-on safety pin spinners, to transform the jig into a small spinnerbait or jig spinner. Finally, when rigging a soft plastic bait on a jig, place a drop or two of Super Glue on the hook shank and under the head where the plastic butts up against lead. This secures the bait firmly in place, where it might otherwise slip off the hook.

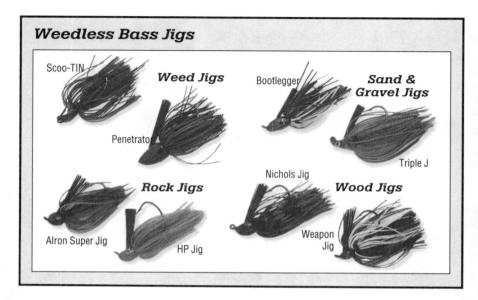

Weedless Bass Jigs

Weed Jigs

Scoo-TIN

Penetrator

Bootlegger

Sand & Gravel Jigs

Triple J

Rock Jigs

Nichols Jig

Wood Jigs

Alron Super Jig

HP Jig

Weapon Jig

FISHING A JIG AND ARTIFICIAL COMBO

Where & When—Artificial-jig combos work well when fish position near cover, such as weeds and wood, particularly in shallow water. In weeds, where you might otherwise tear livebait off the hook, plastics can be aggressively ripped through the vegetation. Lots of times, too, small panfish pester and steal livebait. Jig and artificial combos provide the answer. Jigs coupled with artificial baits work much better than jig and bait combos for repeated casting and retrieving, as there's no need to worry about damaging the bait or casting it off the hook. And many anglers travel to waters where livebait (or at least live minnows) is prohibited, making plastics a top option. In most Canadian waters, you'll catch walleyes and most other species on artificial jigs.

Presentation—In comparison to jigs tipped with livebait, jig and plastic combos can be worked much more aggressively. You can impart hops, pops, and forward sweeps to the jig. When in doubt about whether a strike has occurred, set the hook immediately. To understand the basic process, start in shallow water. Standing on a dock or in a boat, pitch a jig maybe 30 feet out into 3 to 6 feet of water. Engage the reel. Now, immediately begin watching your line—probably the most critical aspect of jig fishing. When the jig contacts bottom, you'll see the line stop moving and suddenly go slack. Point the rod tip just above the jig and then move the rod toward 1 o'clock to hop the jig off bottom. Reel slowly as you drop the rod back toward 2:30, then stop again. The jig settles back toward bottom, fluttering toward you as it descends. Watch the line go slack again. Repeat the lift-drop until the jig is under the boat.

Pork And Plastic Trailers For Bass Jigs

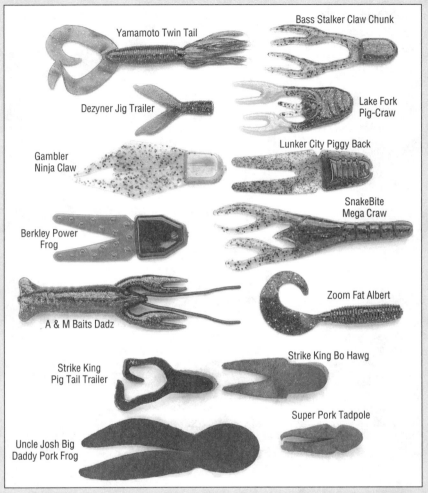

Yamamoto Twin Tail

Bass Stalker Claw Chunk

Dezyner Jig Trailer

Lake Fork Pig-Craw

Gambler Ninja Claw

Lunker City Piggy Back

SnakeBite Mega Craw

Berkley Power Frog

A & M Baits Dadz

Zoom Fat Albert

Strike King Pig Tail Trailer

Strike King Bo Hawg

Super Pork Tadpole

Uncle Josh Big Daddy Pork Frog

Though plastic has dethroned pork rind as the most popular type of trailer for bass jigs, pork remains a valuable option in many situations. Its undulating action makes it ideal in cold water or for non-aggressive fish. And its tough hide performs well when fishing around boat docks, dense emergent grass, or timber.

Panfish Heads

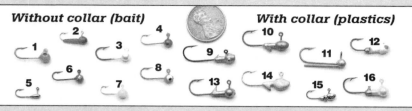

Without collar (bait)   **With collar (plastics)**

Without collar: (1) Mister Twister; (2) Custom Jigs N' Spins Rat Finkee; (3) Jigg's World Of Jigs; (4) Shearwater Tackle; (5) Turner Jones Micro Tube Jig; (6) Thunderhawk Mean E; (7) Jack's Jigs; (8) Incredible Bait Bergie Head. **With collar:** 9) Owner Jig; (10) Creme Tube Jig; (11) Bass Pro Shops Crosseyed Jighead; (12) Blue Fox Boxee Jig; (13) Mister Twister; (14) Kalin; (15) Turner Jones Micro Lure; (16) Jigg's World of Jigs.

Panfish Plastics

Tubes   **Grubs**   **Worms**   **Craws**   **Auger Tails**   **Specialty**

Tubes top to bottom: Berkley Micro; Creme Tube; Kalin Tube; Bass Pro Shops Salty Squirmin' Squirt; Bobbie Garland Crappie Tube. **Grubs top to bottom:** Comet Spike; Thunderhawk Mean-E Grub; Berkley Power Wiggler; Fish Hawk Split Tail; Blue Fox Foxee; Bass Pro Shops Marabou Squirt. **Worms top to bottom:** Bergie Worm; Bergie Worm; Berkley Micro Sand Worm; Berkley 3" Power Worm. **Craws top to bottom:** Berkley Micro Craw; Bass Pro Shops Lil'Squirt Craw; Riverside micro Air Craw. **Auger Tails top to bottom:** Thunderhawk Mean-E Spin; Mister Twister; Lind-Little Joe Swirl Tail; Kalin Hologram Tail; Riverside Micro Air Grub. **Specialty top to bottom:** Bergie Leech; Cubby Jig; Creme Lit'L Fishee; Riverside Micro Air Lizard.

Panfish Hair Jigs

(1) Rainbow Lures Mini Jig; (2) Andy's Panfish Hair Jig; (3) Bass Pro Shops Crappie Jig; (4) Hal Fly; (5) Turner Micro Lure; (6) Fle-Fly; (7) Stumpy Bayou; (8) Northland Gypsy Jig; (9) Blue Fox Big Crappie Jig; (10) Northland Fire-Fly Jig; (11) Lindy-Little Joe; (12) Mister Twister Crappie Jig; (13) Cabela's Feather Bug; (14) Mister Twister Lightnin' Bug; (15) Cabela's Trout Jig; (16) Fish Hawk Slo Slicker; (17) Wazp Bug.

European Rigs

QUICK-STRIKE RIGGING & MUCH MORE

In the mid 1980s, when In-Fisherman introduced quick-strike rigging to North America, European fishermen had already been using similar rigs for many years. With long rods, they could propel baits over 100 yards from shore, using small hooks to rig large baitfish for giant pike, zander (a European cousin of the walleye), and wels catfish. English waters—small lakes, ponds, and canals—often contain super-selective fish, well beyond North American standards. Yet these anglers were catching, safely releasing, and catching the same fish many times.

PRIMARY SPECIES _____

TACKLE

Rod & Reel—A fast-action, medium-heavy-power spinning rod 8 to 12 feet long teams well with quick-strike rigs, particularly with floats. A large-capacity spinning reel with a longcast spool matches long rods.

Main Line—8- to 20-pound-test monofilament or superline.

Sinker—Depends on bait size and casting distance.

Connections—A single barrel or ball-bearing swivel attaches to the end of the quick-strike leader, which reduces line twist and provides a handy connection point for the main line. To create an adjustable-hook rig, slide a short piece of plastic tubing over the shank of the second hook and leader. The tubing holds the hook in place when placed in a bait, but easily can be moved up or down the line to accommodate different sized baits.

Leader—A quick-strike rig typically consists of an 8- to 18-inch section of 18- to 27-pound stranded wire, as sharp-toothed pike and muskies are primary targets. Other line materials, such as mono, can also be used for other species.

Knots—For securing stranded wire to hooks and swivels, line is wrapped rather than knotted. Wire can also be firmed in place by sliding a small metal sleeve over the main and tag ends, securing it in place with crimping pliers. When tying the rig with mono, hooks can be secured with snell knots and the swivel with a Trilene knot.

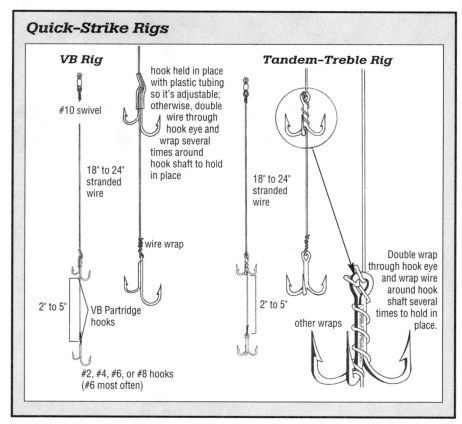

Quick-Strike Rigs

VB Rig

#10 swivel

18" to 24" stranded wire

hook held in place with plastic tubing so it's adjustable; otherwise, double wire through hook eye and wrap several times around hook shaft to hold in place

wire wrap

2" to 5"

VB Partridge hooks

#2, #4, #6, or #8 hooks (#6 most often)

Tandem-Treble Rig

18" to 24" stranded wire

2" to 5"

other wraps

Double wrap through hook eye and wrap wire around hook shaft several times to hold in place.

Making Quick-Strike Rigs With Monofilament

1. Insert leader 13 to 15 inches.

VB hook with
turned-down eye

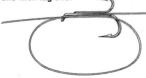

Tie the lead hook first. Run about 14 inches of line through the down-turned eye of the VB hook from the eye toward the barbs.

2. Form loop.

Form a loop by placing the tail end of the leader along the shank of the hook with about an inch beyond the barbs.

3. Hold leader and loop to hook shank with a one-inch tag end.

Pinch the two lines to the shank.

4. Wrap loop forward around hook shank and leader.

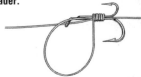

With your other hand, grasp the portion of the loop near the barbs and wind it seven to ten times around the shank from the barb end toward the eye. The wrappings must be in mid-shank; don't wrap over the sharp end of the small, piggyback hook. Make sure the line through the eye lies straight along the shank. If it twists more than a quarter turn while wrapping, slide the wraps around the shank to straighten line.

5. Pull loop through wrappings—you may need to lubricate line with saliva or WD-40.

pull

6. Inspect: leader not twisted or over sharp spot

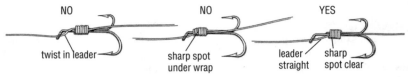

NO — twist in leader

NO — sharp spot under wrap

YES — leader straight — sharp spot clear

7. Snug up snell from both ends

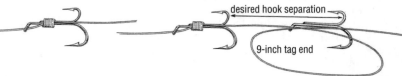

8. Position second hook on tag-end of leader (repeat steps 2 through 7)

desired hook separation

9-inch tag end

Common Bottom-Fishing Deadbait Rigs

Slipsinker Rig

quick-strike rig

main line

egg sinker

Sinker-Forward Rig

main line

12"

bell sinker

12"

Static Deadbait Rig

float

stop knot and bead

distance determined by water depth and line tension

leader

bullet lead

Hooks—Two hooks, rigged in tandem 2 to 4 inches apart, virtually ensure a solid hook-set. Many European anglers use special double hooks designed for quick-strike rigging, but #4 to #8 treble hooks are more available. When using treble hooks, though, some anglers snip the third tine off the shank with a wire cutter, with little loss in hooksetting success.

Natural Baits—The quick-strike rig was created to present large baitfish, dead or alive. In North America, common baits include whole dead rainbow smelt, ciscoes, and herring; or live suckers, creek chubs, shiners, shad, carp, sunfish, and bullheads. When hooking deadbait, insert one hook into the back of the bait just behind the head; the second hook slips into the bait between the tail and the dorsal fin, parallel to the terminal hook. Both hook points should face away from the head, so line trails beyond the tail.

RIGGING WRINKLES

In many states, in order to use a double or treble hook with natural bait, a small spinner must be added to the leader to make the rig into a lure.

FISHING A QUICK-STRIKE RIG

Where & When—When fishing large live or dead baitfish, or when you're having difficulty hooking fish on large baits with single-hook rigs, a quick-strike rig works wonders. The rig's design allows for immediate hooksets—often eliminating worries about deeply hooked fish, which means most fish can be released in fine shape. Across North America, this rig is often employed by ice anglers targeting pike, though it can be used successfully for any fish that eat large baitfish any time of the year.

Presentation—The quick-strike rig can be fished beneath a tip-up while ice fishing, or cast on a rod and reel. In open water, anglers often use the rig with large deadbaits to intercept pike moving to and from shallow spawning bays. Largemouth and striped bass anglers also use the rig baited with large live shiners, shad, eels, and sunfish, often beneath a large slipfloat. Anglers in search of large catfish—particularly flatheads—use a quick-strike rig to hook large live baitfish. Remember, when a fish hits, don't wait or feed line—set the hook immediately.

HAIR RIGS

Curious to the eyes of most American anglers, the hair rig is another ingenious solution to a common fishing dilemma. Unlike most fish, carp—the most widely pursued fish in Europe—use pharyngeal teeth, which lie in the throat to grind food for digestion. Carp also are acknowledged as perhaps the most selective and intelligent freshwater fish. They taste their food prior to eating it. They might gently brush a bait with their lips or sip and then spit a bait too rapidly for most anglers to react. When a carp eats a hair-rigged bait, however, the hook lies in perfect position to find flesh right near the inner lip. In many cases, even when a carp expels a hair-rigged bait, the hook catches flesh on the way out, starting the hook-setting process. While the rig was designed for carp, a little creative thought should yield a host of other species and situations that lend themselves to hair rigging.

PRIMARY SPECIES

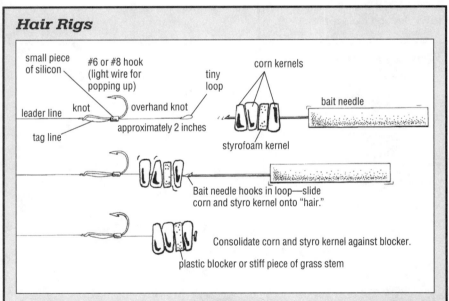

Hair Rigs

Rationale: *The hair rig was originally tied with hair. Carp don't care about the free hook; they don't know what a hook is. They focus on the corn, sucking the kernels into the backs of their mouths. The hook rides free, ready to set into flesh, and almost always rests at the front of a fish's mouth.*
Notes: A snell knot or even an overhand knot works to secure the tag end of the hook shank. Carp find this rig easier to eat, and your hookup percentage is vastly increased. Commercially tied hair rigs are available from Euro Tackle. So are bait needles, dacron, plastic stoppers, and yellow styro (white works too).

TACKLE

Rod & Reel—A 7- to 12-foot, moderately-fast-action, medium-power spinning rod; medium-capacity spinning reel with a longcast spool.

Line—8- to 12-pound-test mono or superline.

Sinker—The hair rig works best when teamed with a three-way or set rig and a bell or bass-casting sinker, or a slipsinker rig with a bell, egg, or walking sinker. The hair can also be fished as a split-shot rig and even drifted near the surface beneath a casting bubble.

Connections—Tie a small swivel to the end of the leader. If fishing the hair on a three-way rig, a three-way swivel should be used.

Leader—Unless you're presenting a bait on the surface, a 12- to 18-inch leader is appropriate. For carp, the leader material should be soft and limp, such as braided dacron or superline. Carp have sensitive mouths, making softer, less-rigid lines more effective; stiff lines might spook carp.

Knots—The simplest method of tying a hair rig is a snell knot. Leave a 2- or 3-inch tag line beyond the hook to serve as the rig's hair. At the end of the hair, tie a small overhand knot, leaving a loop in the line no more than 1/4 inch wide. Once baited, insert a small piece of twig or grass stem into the loop, which keeps bait from sliding off the hair. A piece of rubber band or plastic also can be used as a hair stop.

Hooks—Small light-wire hooks, #10 to #4, best match hair rigging. Octopus or O'Shaughnessy hooks work fine in most situations. Choose hooks with up- or down-turned eyes for snelling.

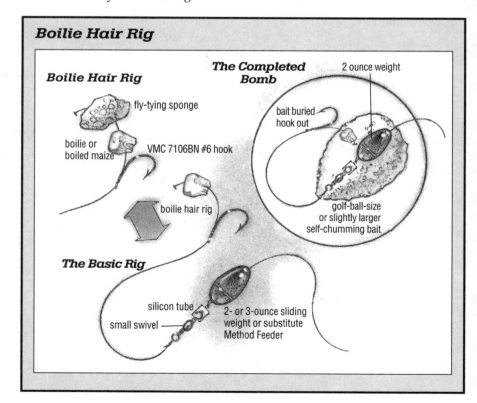

Boilie Hair Rig

Boilie Hair Rig

fly-tying sponge

boilie or boiled maize

VMC 7106BN #6 hook

boilie hair rig

The Completed Bomb

2 ounce weight

bait buried hook out

golf-ball-size or slightly larger self-chumming bait

The Basic Rig

silicon tube

small swivel

2- or 3-ounce sliding weight or substitute Method Feeder

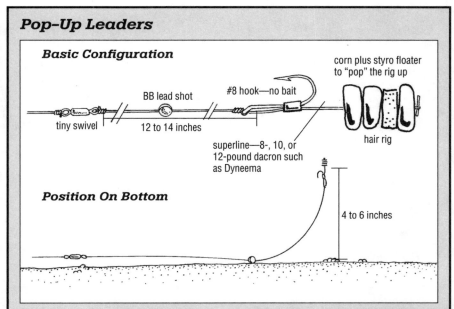

Pop-Up Leaders

Basic Configuration

corn plus styro floater to "pop" the rig up

BB lead shot

#8 hook—no bait

tiny swivel

12 to 14 inches

hair rig

superline—8-, 10, or 12-pound dacron such as Dyneema

Position On Bottom

4 to 6 inches

Note: *Carp have sensitive mouths, thus the soft superline is preferred to stiffer monofilament. Mono works too for most American carp. Keep breakstrengths in the 8-, 10-, 12-, or 14-pound range.*

Rationale: *Free offerings of corn are on the bottom in a baited area. Passing carp see the baited area, become curious, move toward the area, then see individual pieces of corn. Once close, the first thing they see is the rig popped-up above the bottom. It's a little bigger and at mouth level. Perfect!*

Natural Baits—Common baits include sweet corn, peas, and garbanzo beans. Though not usually associated with hair rigging, many other baits, such as small nightcrawlers and waxworms, sometimes work well. When pursuing large carp, the superior bait remains softened field corn. Where legal, chumming your fishing area with bait might improve your catch.

Commercial Baits—Various types of doughbaits work well on a hair rig. Slide a bead or small piece of cork onto the hair, then mold the dough around it. A round, hardened doughbait, called a boilie, remains the most popular and effective bait for carp in Europe.

RIGGING WRINKLES

A bait needle is essential for threading bait onto a hair rig. Bait needles aren't readily available in North America, but a straightened #2 Aberdeen hook functions well as a substitute. When rigging corn, push several kernels onto the needle, catch the barb on the hair loop, then slide the corn from the needle to the line. Some anglers prefer to "pop up" or float the hair rig off the bottom to better attract attention to their offering. This is achieved by adding one or two small bits of styrofoam onto the hair along with the bait. Finally, to better keep the hair and bait trailing straight behind the hook, slip a 1/4-inch section of clear silicon tubing over the line and hook, near the bend.

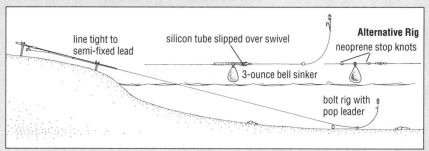

The Bolt Rig (Semi-Fixed)

line tight to semi-fixed lead

silicon tube slipped over swivel

Alternative Rig
neoprene stop knots

3-ounce bell sinker

bolt rig with pop leader

A bolt rig consists of a fixed or semi-fixed lead of at least 3 ounces in conjunction with a short leader. The carp picks up the baited hook, feels resistance, and "bolts" off, setting the "free" hook in the process. Just lift the rod and hang on. At least 3 ounces of lead is needed to accomplish the set.

The English use a semi-fixed rig as a conservation measure. If the lead is permanently attached to the leader and the line breaks, the carp ends up dragging around the lead. If it gets stuck in rocks and the fish can't break free, the fish starves.

FISHING A HAIR RIG

Where & When—Anytime you're stillfishing baits over clean bottom areas, a hair rig might be appropriate. Remember, the rig isn't just for carp, but for any fish that feeds near bottom. The rig also is helpful when fish take baits deeply.

Presentation—Most anglers prefer to fish the hair rig while casting from shore. Cast it into water you believe holds feeding fish, place the rod in a rod holder, and wait. To bring fish into your area, consider tossing a few handfuls of bait (chum) into the water. When a fish takes, reel in slack line and immediately set the hook.

THE FLOAT PATERNOSTER RIG

Essentially the combination of a slipfloat and three-way sliprig, the float paternoster rig fills a few key niches in fishing. While a slipfloat rig drifts with wind and current, holding baits above snags, the three-way fishes well as a stationary rig but becomes easily snagged in weeds or wood. The float paternoster rig offers a compromise, allowing you to set a bait in a key spot without worrying about it drifting away from the desired location or into snags.

PRIMARY SPECIES

TACKLE

Rod & Reel—A 7- to 10-foot, moderately-fast-action, medium- to heavy-power casting rod; medium- to large-capacity casting reel.

Line—8- to 30-pound-test, abrasion-resistant monofilament or superline.

Sinker—A fairly heavy bell sinker anchors the float paternoster rig—1/2 to 3 ounces or more depending on bait size, depth, and current. Like the three-way rig, the sinker lies at the base of a dropper line, which should be of a lighter break strength than the main line to allow it to break off in snags, freeing the remainder of the rig. Dropper length also determines the distance between the bait and the bottom.

Connections—Use a three-way swivel or two separate barrel swivels to build this rig. Barrel swivels let the main line slip, allowing livebaits more freedom and letting fish run unencumbered by weight. The three-way swivel may be preferable when fishing in tighter quarters near snags, as it better pins a bait in place.

Leader—An 8- to 12-inch leader between main line and bait is standard. Go shorter to restrain baits or to keep them from snagging in heavy cover. Longer leaders allow baits to roam freely, particularly where snags aren't a problem. Near cover, use a superline leader; in super-clear water, consider fluorocarbon.

Knots—The Trilene knot is a fine choice for line-to-swivel and line-to-sinker connections. Consider a snell knot for connecting the hook to the leader. A float stop knot also needs to be tied for this rig.

Hooks—Most float paternoster applications involve large livebaits; therefore, #2 to 6/0 and larger hooks are usually needed. Choose hooks that are durable and with a wide gap. When rigging baits for catfish, a circle hook is a good choice.

Float—The float on this rig need not suspend the entire weight of the rig above bottom, so use a smaller float than you might expect. If you're using a large wild bait, though, use a float that remains buoyant even under tow by the bait. Medium to large cigar-shaped floats are a top choice.

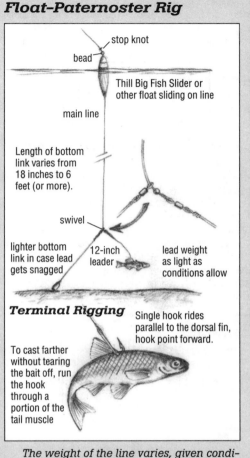

Float–Paternoster Rig

stop knot

bead

Thill Big Fish Slider or other float sliding on line

main line

Length of bottom link varies from 18 inches to 6 feet (or more).

swivel

lighter bottom link in case lead gets snagged

12-inch leader

lead weight as light as conditions allow

Terminal Rigging

Single hook rides parallel to the dorsal fin, hook point forward.

To cast farther without tearing the bait off, run the hook through a portion of the tail muscle

The weight of the line varies, given conditions. For big flatheads in reservoirs where snags aren't a problem, run 30-pound main line and a 20-pound bottom link. When channel cats are the target in a similar environment, drop to 17- or 20-pound main line and a 14-pound bottom link. For 40- to over 50-pound cats in snaggy water, run at least 50-pound main line and a 20-pound link.

Natural Baits—Large live baitfish—suckers, chubs, shad, bullheads, and sunfish—swim well beneath a paternoster rig. Big lively baits work best because the rig remains set in place, relying heavily on the natural attracting power of a vigorous bait—the bait calls the fish to the rig. Most natural baits, when applied to the right species and situation, catch fish on a float-paternoster rig.

RIGGING WRINKLES

Adding an additional leader to the main line beneath the float allows you to fish two different baits at different depths. Slide the leader down the line on a swivel to a small split shot or additional stop knot, which determines the depth.

FISHING A FLOAT-PATERNOSTER RIG

Where & When—The float-paternoster rig excels as a shorefishing rig, especially to position a bait within a small area—particularly an area surrounded by cover such as brushpiles, wood, or weeds that harbor catfish, bass, pike, and other fish. By using a sufficiently heavy sinker, the rig remains set firmly in place, which is particularly important in rivers when any amount of downstream drag means an instant snag. So the paternoster gives you the vertical presentation of a slipfloat rig, combined with the stationary holding power of a three-way set rig.

Presentation—While fishing from shore or an anchored boat, target a precise area with your cast. It's important to know the depth of the spot you're fishing—at least within a general range. If the water is 5 feet deep, for instance, set the slipfloat stop knot just beyond 5 feet above the bell sinker. Set shallower, the float will sink. Set deeper, the bait is allowed a wider range of movement, which can be a fine idea when trying to attract fish from greater distances. Providing too much play between sinker and float, though, allows both the float and the bait to drift into snags. To determine the right depth for the situation, boat anglers often hover directly over the fishing area and drop the rig to the bottom, where they can make immediate and precise adjustments of the bobber stop. Once depth is set, drop the rig onto the spot, motor away and anchor or beach the boat on shore while awaiting the first strike.

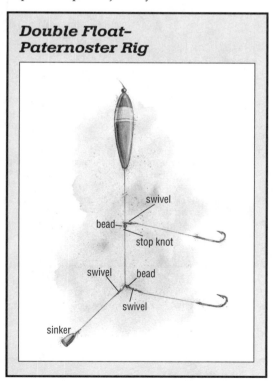

Double Float-Paternoster Rig

swivel

bead

stop knot

swivel   bead

swivel

sinker

Presentation Pointers

BAIT, RODS, REELS, LINE, HOOKS & MORE

Considering the many kinds of fish and diverse ways to catch them can be mind-boggling. In this chapter, we look in detail at tools of the trade—baits, hooks, sinkers, floats, lines, soft-plastic lures, with our recommendations on good combinations for every sort of fishing situation.

Blue Catfish—dead whole or cut sections of gizzard shad, skipjack herring, white sucker, freshwater clams, nightcrawlers, chicken entrails.

Carp—insect larvae, waxworms, small crayfish, freshwater clams, sweet corn.

Chain Pickerel—small to medium shiners, suckers, chubs, sunfish.

Channel Catfish—chubs, suckers, nightcrawlers, ribbon leeches, grasshoppers, leopard frogs, crayfish, freshwater clams, chicken entrails, congealed beef and poultry blood; dead sections of sucker, chub, goldeye, shad, carp.

Crappies—small shiners and fathead minnows, waxworms, insect larvae.

Flathead Catfish—large live chubs, suckers, bullheads, carp, sunfish.

Lake Trout—suckers, shiners, chubs; dead whole smelt, ciscoes, suckers.

Largemouth Bass—suckers, nightcrawlers, ribbon leeches, crayfish, waterdogs, leopard frogs.

Muskellunge—suckers.

Northern Pike—suckers, chubs, waterdogs, leopard frogs; dead smelt, ciscoes, suckers.

Salmon & Stream Trout—sculpin, suckers, shiners, fatheads, grasshoppers, mayfly nymphs, waxworms, mealworms, salmon eggs, nightcrawlers, angleworms, small crayfish, freshwater and grass shrimp.

Smallmouth Bass—shiners, chubs, ribbon leeches, nightcrawlers, crayfish.

Striped Bass & Wipers—gizzard shad, shiners, sunfish, eels; dead anchovy, alewives, stripers.

Sunfish & Perch—angleworms, nightcrawler pieces, ribbon leeches, waxworms, small minnows, crickets.

Walleye—ribbon leeches, nightcrawlers, shiners, chubs, fatheads, waterdogs, leopard frogs.

Soft Plastics For Every Situation

Walleye Plastics

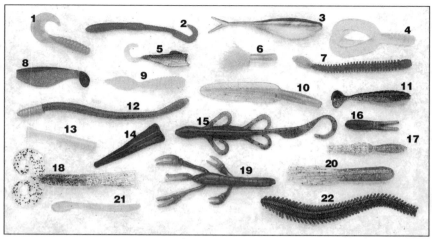

(1) Curlytail Grubs; (2) Curlytail Worms; (3) Jerk Shads; (4) Twintails; (5) Minnows; (6) Marabou-Tail Grubs; (7) Ribbed Worms; (8) Shads; (9) Sting Ray Grubs; (10) Reapers; (11) Paddletail Grubs; (12) Straighttail Worms; (13) Nail-Tail Grubs; (14) Leeches; (15) Lizards; (16) Splittail Grubs; (17) Solid Tubes; (18) Spider Grubs; (19) Crawfish; (20) Hollow Tubes; (21) Jigworms; (22) Leggy Tails.

Panfish Plastics

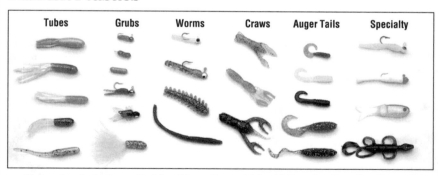

Tubes top to bottom: *Berkley Micro; Creme Tube; Kalin tube; Bass Pro Shops Salty Squirmin' Squirt; Bobbie Garland Crappie Tube.* **Grubs:** *Comet Spike; Thunderhawk Mean-E Grub; Berkley Power Wiggler; Fish Hawk Split Tail; Blue Fox Foxee; Bass Pro Shops Maribou Squirt.* **Worms:** *Bergie Worm; Bergie Worm; Berkley Micro Sand Worm Berkley 3" Power Worm.* **Craws:** *Berkley Micro Craw; Bass Pro Shops Lil' Squirt Craw; Riverside Micro Air Craw.* **Auger Tails:** *Thunderhawk Mean-E Spin; Mister Twister; Lindy-Little Joe Swirl Tail; Kalin Hologram Tail; Riverside Micro Air Grub.* **Specialty:** *Bergie Leech; Cubby Jig; Creme Lit'L Fishee; Riverside Micro Air Lizard.*

Selected Bass Plastics

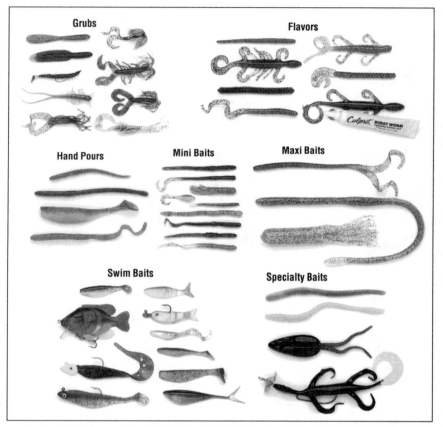

Grubs • Flavors • Hand Pours • Mini Baits • Maxi Baits • Swim Baits • Specialty Baits

Grubs: 1st Column—Angler's Choice Split-Tail Beaver; Iovino Scalpie; Charlie Brewer Bass Grub Lunker City Hellgie; Yamamoto Hula Grub; ReAction Double Take Skirted Grub; Arkie Salty Crawlin' Grub; 2nd Column—Zorro Hoot-N-Ninny; Kalin Mop Top. **Flavors:** 1st Column—Angler's Choice worm with Alive formula; Arkie Salty Crawlin' Lizard; Zetabait Ringo with menhaden oil; V & M 2 Twist with pork fat; 2nd Column— Bass Assassin Lizard with Hog Lard and P Enzyme; Berkley NEONZ with new Power-Bait formula; Culprit Burst Lizard. **Hand Pours:** Iovino Finesse worm; Kalin Hand Pour; AA Swim Bait; Preferred Plastics 7-inch worm. **Mini Baits:** Iovino Finesse worm; AA Curl Tail Worm; Iovino Split-Shot Fatzee; Bass Assassin Curly Shad; Angler's Choice 3-inch worm; Zetabait Illusion; Mister Twister 4-inch Phenom; Charlie Brewer Slider worm; Kalin Salty Finesse Worm. **Maxi Baits:** ReAction 10-inch Double Take; AA 16-inch worm; Canyon Tora Tube. **Swim Baits:** 1st Column—Mister Twister Sassy Shad; Castaic Sun Fish; Mister Wiffle; AA Swim Bait; 2nd Column—Luck "E: Strike The Slice; Creme Lit'l Fishie; Bass Assassin Curly Shad; Bass Assassin Turbo Shad; Kalin Swim Bait; Lunker City Fin-S Shad. **Specialty Baits:** Carolina Fish & Fur Original Floater; Zoom Trick Worm; Mister Twister Jerk Rat; Buzzin Lizzie.

Guide To Jigs 'N Plastic Combos

Mood/ Activity Level	Inactive	Neutral
Retrieve Speed	Stationary to slow drag or lift-drop.	Slow to medium lift-drop and drag; medium drag-hop and glide; slow swimming.
Jighead Design	Walking, dragging, standup.	Standard round head (ball-head); standard bullet head.
Jig Weight *general guidelines:*	Weight depends on depth fished and retrieve speed; 1/16 to 1/4 ounce	1/8 to 5/8 ounce
Tail Length	2" to 3"	2" to 4"
Tail Design/Action	No tail; straight tail; tube; grub body; with tentacles; hair or feather tail.	Swimming tail; grub body with tentacles.
Water Clarity	Use subtle, natural colors in clear water and bright colors ir dark water. In stained water, try something in between.	
Tail Color	*Clear Water* Yellow, white, black, brown, green smoke, clear, glitter, subtle two-tones.	*Stained Water* Depends on degree of stain. Begin with brighter, dark-water colors or two-tone tails

Inactive   Neutral

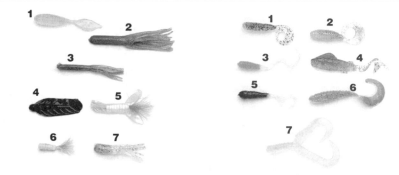

Inactive: (1) Mann's Sting Ray Grub; (2) Berkley Power Tube; (3) Stanley Gitzit; (4) Berkley Power Leech; (5) Blue Fox Foxee; (6) Lindy-Little Joe Glow Fuzz-E-Grub; (7) Northland Tackle Gum-Drop. **Neutral:** (1) Mann's Manipulator Grub; (2) Kalin's Triple Threat Grub; (3) Bass Pro Shops Triple Ripple Grub; (4) Mister Twister Sassy Shiner; (5) Berkley Power Grub; (6) Mister Twister Meeny Tail Grub; (7) Mister Twister Double Tail.

Active

Medium swimming or gliding; medium-fast lift-drop.

Swimming; gliding; propeller; tail spinner jigs.

1/4 to 3/4 ounce plus

3" to 5"+

Swimming, gliding, or thumper tails.

Dark Water

Chartreuse, fluorescent orange, neon, phosphorescent, metallic, bright two-tones.

Active

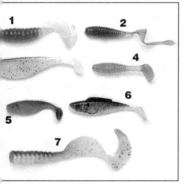

Active: (1) Berkley Power Grub; (2) Mann's Auger-Tail Grub; (3) Culprit Shad Tail Grub; (4) Mann's Swimmin' Grub; (5) Mister Twister Sassy Shad; (6) Renosky Super Shad; (7) 6" Kalin's Mogambo Grub.

Big Plastics For Pike, Muskie, & Stripers

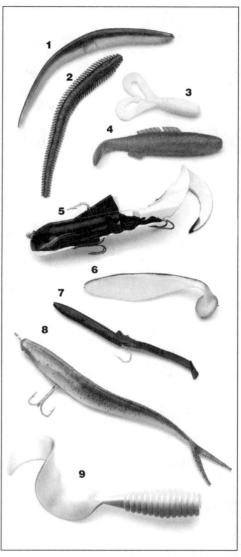

(1) Lunker City 9" Slug-Go; (2) Berkley Power sand Worm; (3) Bass Pro Shrimpi; (4) Berkley Power Shiner; (5) Musky Innovations' Bull Dawg; (6) Mister Twister 6" Bigwater Shad; (7) Blu Fox Raglou Sand Eel; (8) Lunker City 10" Fin-S Fish; (9) Kalin Bug'Un Saltwater Grub.

Categorizing Rod Options

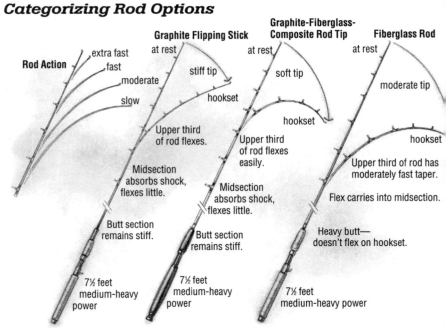

Action is the bend of the rod; power, the strength of the rod: related, but not the same. Mos rods designed for lure presentations have fast tips; those designed for natural bait have slowe actions. Many traditional catfishing presentations call for rods with moderate tips and suff cient power to land heavy fish. Other situations—tightlining, drifting, and using circle hook to name a few—are better met with moderate- to fast-action rods with a light tip.

Rod Grips

Pistol Grip

Length: 5½ to 6 feet

Weight and Power: mostly medium and medium-heavy, although the range is from medium-light to heavy. **Action:** medium to extra-fast. **Comments:** Pistol grips mostly of cork. Rods mostly graphite; two companies offer boron in this and other categories.

Triggerstick

Length: 6 to 7 fe

Weight and Power: mostly medium and medium-heavy, although the range is from medium-light to heavy. **Action:** medium to extra-fast. **Comments** popular "new" category. Mostly straight handles, longer handles for two-handed casts. Fiberglass models available for crankin'.

Spinning

Length: 5 to 7 feet; most rods are 6

Weight and Power: medium-light to heavy; preference for medium to medium-heavy rods. **Action:** almost entirely fast action. **Comments:** Critical for many finesse presentations. The medium power and weight, fas action 6-foot jigging rod is one of the finest rods marketed by most companies.

Rod Mechanics When Fighting A Fish

Torque

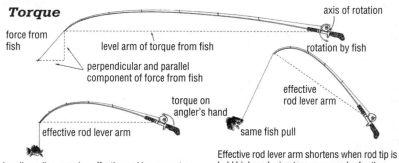

axis of rotation

force from fish

level arm of torque from fish

rotation by fish

perpendicular and parallel component of force from fish

effective rod lever arm

torque on angler's hand

effective rod lever arm

same fish pull

Fish pulls on line, causing effective rod lever arm to twist or torque angler's hand. Conversely, angler applies large lifting torque, causing small force on fish.

Effective rod lever arm shortens when rod tip is held high, reducing torque on angler for the same fish pull—allows angler to apply larger lifting torque and force on fish.

Rod Length And Torque

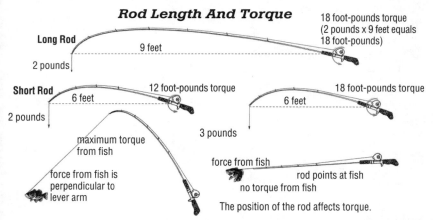

Long Rod

9 feet

2 pounds

18 foot-pounds torque (2 pounds x 9 feet equals 18 foot-pounds)

Short Rod

6 feet

12 foot-pounds torque

18 foot-pounds torque

2 pounds

6 feet

3 pounds

maximum torque from fish

force from fish is perpendicular to lever arm

force from fish

rod points at fish

no torque from fish

The position of the rod affects torque.

For a given fish–pulling force at the rod tip, a short rod puts less torque on you, allowing you to increase the drag force and your lifting force for a higher tip force on the fish. You can pull the fish in faster with a short rod. But short rods are not always the best choice for the varieties of fishing situations you'll face.

itchin'

Length: 6½ to 7½ feet

eight and Power: medium to heavy. **Action:** mostly edium-fast, although range is from medium to extra- st. **Comments:** 7½-foot medium to medium-heavy chin' sticks with medium-fast actions are used for th pitchin' and flippin'. One rod does double duty.

Flippin'

Length: 7 to 8 feet

Weight and Power: mostly medium-heavy and heavy, ranging to extra-heavy. **Action:** mostly medium-fast action. **Comments:** Heavy flippin' sticks tend to be reserved for heavy cover. The trend is toward a 7-foot flippin' stick for both pitchin' and flippin'.

Lines (Mono, Braids, Superlines, & More)

Matching Line With Technique

Key

Gear—S=spinning	AR—abrasion resistant	TS—thin high-tensile
C=casting	HV—high visibility	strength
AP—all-purpose	LC—limp, castable	T—trolling

Technique	Gear	Terrain	Line Type	Pound Test
Backtrolling jigs	S	rock	AR	6-10
Backtrolling bait rigs	S	rock	main:TS/AP	6-8
		rock	leader:AR	6-8
Backtrolling bait rigs	S	sand	Main:LC/AP	6-8
		sand	leader:LC	4-6
Backtrolling-spinner rigs	S	sand	main: LC/AP	6-8
		sand	leader:AR	6-8
Bottom bouncing	C	any	main:AR	12-15
		any	leader:AR	8-12
Casting crankbaits	S or C	any	LC/TS/AP	6-10
Casting jigs	S	rock	AR/HV	6-12
Casting jigs	S	sand	LC/HV/AP	4-8
Dead sticking	S	gravel	AR/HV/AP	6-8
Float fishing	S	weeds	LC/TS/AP	4-8
Trolling—longline crankbaits	S	any	T/AR	8-15
Trolling—downriggers	C	any	T/AR	8-15
Trolling—planer boards	C	any	T/AR	8-15
Trolling—planer/divers	C	any	T	15-20
Vertical jigging	S	river	TS	6-12

Stiff Lines
1. Transmit vibration better
2. Set hooks faster
3. Set larger hooks better
4. Coil in cold weather
5. Abrades less
6. Increase bottom feel
7. Move less freely in current
8. Tend to accept less shock
9. Allow fish to feel you quicker with livebait rigs
10. Free you from tying more knots

Limp Lines
1. Present livebaits more naturally
2. Require thinner hooks
3. Cast farther
4. Remain supple in cold weather
5. Abrades more easily
6. Slightly reduce bottom feel and lure action
7. Allow current to move a bait freely
8. Buffer shock better
9. Allow slightly more time before fish feel rod pressure
10. Force you to check knots and line often

Line Categories

Line Type	Abbreviation	Market Examples
Abrasion-Resistant	AR	Ande Premium, Berkley XT, Berkley Big Game Inshore, Cortland Camo, Maxima Ultragreen, Super Silver Thread, Stren Super Tough, Triple Fish
Copolymers	C	Berkley Trilene Ultrathin, Cabela's Platinum, Damyl Tectan, Stren Magnathin
Limp, Castable	L	Ande Tournament, Berkley XL, Bass Pro Shops Excel, Fenwick Flexline, Silver Thread Excalibur, Stren Easy Cast
Superbraids	SB	Berkley Gorilla Braid, Cabela's Ripcord, Spiderwire, Suffix Herculine
Fused Braids	FB	Berkley FireLine, Spiderwire Fusion, Cabela's Ripcord SI, Suffix Micro
High Vis	HV	Chartreuse Ande, Berkley XT Solar, yellow Stren, any fluorescent line
Low Vis	LV	Cortland Camo, Fin-Nor Fluorocarbon, Suffix Fluorolon, Triple Fish Camo Escent, VMC Water King, any green or smoke-colored line
Low-Stretch Mono	LS	Gamakatsu G-Power, Spiderwire Mono, Stren Sensor
UV Resistant	UV	Fenwick Flexline, Fenwick Riverline, Silver Thread Excalibur, VMC Water King

Stretch Factors

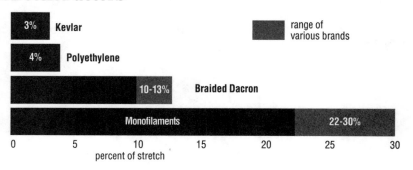

Knots—The Critical Connection

Uni Knot

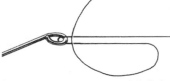

1. Insert tag end through eye, leaving at least 6 inches of line to tie the knot. Double the line and form a loop back toward the eye.

2. Wrap tag end around doubled line and through loop; make 6 turns with light line (2- to 6-pound-test) 5 turns with medium line (8- to 10-pound-test), 4 turns with heavy line (12- to 20-pound-test).

3. Grip tag end; pull slowly to draw knot up semitight.

4. Grip standing line; pull slowly to slide knot formed in Step 3 against eye, drawing it up snugly; trim tag end.

Back To Back Uni-Knots

1. Form a loop with the tag end of the backing and make five wraps around both lines. Repeat with tag end of main line.

2. Pull the tag ends until the knots are tight.

3. Pull both lines to draw the knots together. Trim tag ends close to knot.

Double Line Loop Uni-Knot

1. Double the line and insert in the eye of the hook.

2. Run the line through again.

3. Pull tight, leaving an 18-inch tag end.

4. Form a loop in the tag.

5 & 6. Wrap the tag around the main line and back through the loop five times.

7. Wet the line and pull tight.

8 & 9. Wet the line again and slide the knot to the desired position.

Palomar Knot

1. Double about 4 inches of line and pass the loop through the eye.

2. Let the hook hang loose and tie an overhand knot in the doubled line. Avoid twisting the lines and don't tighten the knot.

3. Pull a loop of line far enough to pass it over the hook, swivel, or lure. Make sure the loop passes completely over this attachment.

4. Pull both tag end and standing line to tighten. Clip at about 1/8 inch.

Triple Palomar Knot

1. Double the line and pass the loop through the eye.

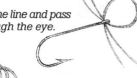

2. Repeat this step twice so three loops of doubled line are formed.

3. Tighten the loops around the eye of the hook, then wrap the doubled line around the main line and tag, forming an overhand knot.

4. Loop the doubled line over the hook.

5. Pull on the main and tag lines to tighten the knot, then trim the tag.

Trilene Knot

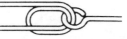

1. Run the end of your line through the eye of the hook or lure twice.

2. Loop around standing part of line 6 times for lines up to 10-pound-test; 5 times for lines testing 12 to 14 pounds; 4 times for heavier lines.

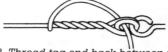

3. Thread tag end back between the eye and the coils.

4. Lubricate, then pull tight and trim tag end.

Albright Knot

1. Bend a loop in the tag end of wire and hold between thumb and forefinger of left hand. Insert the tag end of the lighter line through the loop from the top.

2. Slip tag end of lighter line under your left thumb and pinch it tightly against the heavier strands of the loop. Wrap the first turn of the lighter line over itself and continue wrapping toward the round end of the loop. Take at least 2 turns with the lighter line around all three strands.

3. Insert tag end of the lighter line through end of the loop from the bottom. It must enter and leave the loop on the same side.

4. With the thumb and forefinger of the left hand, slide the coils of the lighter line toward the end of the loop, stopping 1/8 inch from end of loop. Using pliers, pull the tag end of the lighter line tight to keep the coils from slipping off the loop.

5. With your left hand still holding the heavier mono, pull on the standing part of the lighter mono. Pull the tag end of the lighter line and the standing part a second time. Pull the standing part of the wire and the standing part of the light line.

6. Trim both tag ends.

Improved Blood Knot

1. Overlap the ends of your two strands that are to be joined and twist them together about 10 turns.

2. Separate one of the center twists and thrust the two ends through the space as illustrated.

3. Pull knot together and trim off the short ends.

Improved Clinch Knot

1. Insert tag end through eye leaving at least 6 inches of line to tie the knot. Wrap tag end around standing line; make 6 turns with light line (2- to 6-pound-test), 5 turns with medium line (8- to 12-pound-test), 4 turns with heavy line (14- to 20-pound-test). Pass end through loop formed at eye.

2. Insert tag end back through second loop formed in step 1.

3. Maintain tension on tag end; draw knot tight by pulling on standing line; trim tag end.

World's Fair Knot

1. Double a 6-inch length of line and pass the loop through the eye.

2. Bring loop back next to the doubled line; grasp the doubled line through the loop.

3. Pass tag end through the new loop formed by the doubled line.

4. Pass tag end through second loop formed in Step 3; grip tag end; pull to draw knot tight.

5. Pull the tag end snug, slide knot up tight.

Arbor Knot

1. Pull tight on tag end and trim close to knot.

2. Pull on backing to draw knot tight.

monofilament backing to spool

The Quick Uni

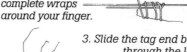

1. Draw the line through and rest it and the main line on your trigger finger, leaving about 8 inches of tag end beyond your finger.

2. Make three complete wraps around your finger.

3. Slide the tag end back through the loop (towards you).

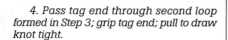

4. Draw the line up.

5. Slide the knot up to the hookeye and trim.

Crawford Knot

1. Insert tag end through eye leaving at least 8 inches of line to tie the knot.

2. Pass tag end around loop formed in Step 1.

3. Pass tag end across front of loop forming a figure eight.

4. Pass tag end between top of loop and standing line; grip tag end; draw knot semitight.

5. Grip standing line and slowly draw knot against eye; trim tag end.

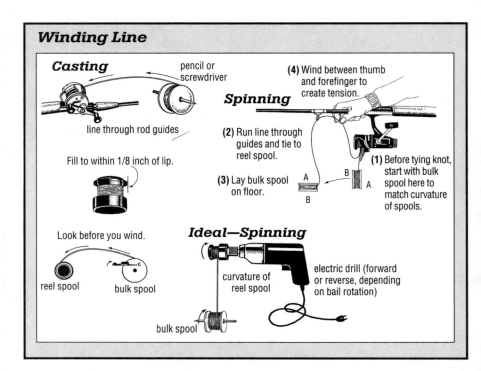

Winding Line

Casting

pencil or screwdriver

line through rod guides

Fill to within 1/8 inch of lip.

Look before you wind.

reel spool   bulk spool

Spinning

(4) Wind between thumb and forefinger to create tension.

(2) Run line through guides and tie to reel spool.

(3) Lay bulk spool on floor.

(1) Before tying knot, start with bulk spool here to match curvature of spools.

A   B   A   B

Ideal—Spinning

curvature of reel spool

electric drill (forward or reverse, depending on bail rotation)

bulk spool

Knot Strength

	LINE SIZE—LABEL-RATED BREAK STRENGTH			
	4 pound	8 pound	12 pound	17 pound
Crawford	86.3%	88.6%	84.3%	79.2%
Improved Clinch	89.7%	94.4%	88.1%	87.0%
Trilene	88.7%	95.1%	89.1%	87.8%
Uni	89.2%	95.8%	78.1%	86.4%
World's Fair	88.7%	94.1%	82.9%	97.2%

Knot Strength Reliability

	LINE SIZE—LABEL RATED BREAK STRENGTH			
	4 pound	8 pound	12 pound	17 pound
Crawford	89.0%	100.0%	63.0%	54.0%
Improved Clinch	94.0%	100.0%	83.0%	94.0%
Trilene	88.7%	100.0%	100.0%	100.0%
Uni	89.2%	100.0%	100.0%	79.0%
World's Fair	88.7%	100.0%	63.0%	72.0%

Wire Connections

Dacron Backing To Wire Line

(A) Make a loop in the wire.

(B) Wrap it 3 or 4 times at the base of the loop.

(C) Make a granny knot above the wraps.

(D) Wrap dacron twice through the loop, leaving a long tag end.

pull

pull

(E) Pull slowly on the wire, the dacron, and both tag ends until the wire knot cinches tight. Be careful not to stress the wire.

snip

Trilene knot

(F) Tie a Trilene knot in the dacron and snip the tag ends.

Sleeves To Connect Wire To Swivels, Bottom Bouncers, & More

(A) Slide sleeve onto wire (#2 sleeve .040).

(B) Loop the end through the swivel twice.

(C) Pull the loop tight and slide the sleeve within 1/8 inch of the swivel.

(D) Crimp the sleeve lightly with a crimping tool.

(E) Test connection—snip tag end tight to sleeve.

Wrapping Wire

(A) Loop the wire twice through the swivel, leaving a 1-inch tag end.

(B) Clip a forceps onto the tag end.

(C) Swing the forceps, spin wrapping the tag end progressively up the main line about an inch. Trim.

Tying Wire

(A) Tie a granny in the wire first. Then slip the tag through the swivel.

(B) Slip the tag through the granny.

(C) And cinch it—but not quite tight.

(D) Loop the tag over the back into the middle of the granny loop.

(E) Pull both ends of the wire to cinch the knot down. Trim the tag end.

To tie wire to dacron, make a tiny loop near the end of the wire, wrap the wire four or five times, and make a loose granny knot below the wraps. Circle the end of the dacron through the tiny loop twice, leaving a long tag end to hold onto. Now slowly pull on the wire and both lines of dacron, cinching the wire down tight. Tie a clinch knot or Trilene knot in the dacron above the wire knot, cut the tag ends of dacron and wire, and cover the connection with a drop of epoxy.

Parts of a Hook

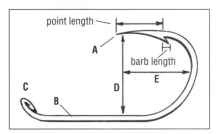

(A) The Point—*Must be sharp. The longer the point, the longer it takes to penetrate. Reduce barbs with a file to ensure quick penetration.*

(B) The Bend and Shank—*Shank wire gauge and weight and hook size must match line weight. A thick-shanked #1 won't sink past the barb if the hookset is fueled by a light-action rod and 4-pound line. Some steel shanks have less torque or bend during* a hookset. Others bend easily. Which you choose depends on the situation.

(C) The Eye—*Eyes are straight, turned down, or turned up. The design determines the knot you use and the rigging application. Turned-up eyes are used for livebait snells, straight eyes for pitching bait coupled with a lead shot. Turned-down eyes are used with crawler rigs.*

(D) Hook Gap—*Critical. Small gaps don't grab and hold as quickly or efficiently as large gaps. Use the largest gap you can get away with. Bending the base of the shank of a hook out 5 to 10 degrees opens the gap enough on some hooks to improve hookups.*

(E) The Throat—*It must be just deep enough to allow flesh to pass the barb. Short's better than long for most walleye applications.*

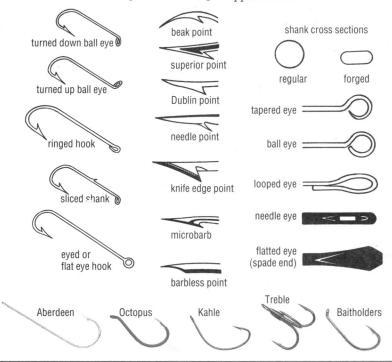

Hook Size

Most fishermen prefer a #8 for leeches and small crawlers, a #6 for crawlers, and a #6 or #4 for minnows. The trend among good fishermen, though, is to use a size or two larger hook when they can get away with it. Increased hook size increases the size of the hook gap, which tends to improve hooking percentage.

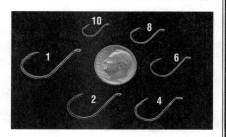

Straight or Offset?

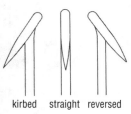

kirbed   straight   reversed

Hooks can be straight or offset. "Kirbed" hooks are offset left; "reversed" hooks are offset right. While a theoretical case can be made for offsetting left instead of right, or vice versa, it has little to do with basic fishing.

Fishermen who prefer offset hooks believe they increase the potential to catch hold. Offset hooks require slightly more force to sink in, however. Other fishermen prefer straight hooks. To ensure high-percentage hooking, some fishermen increase gap size by fishing a larger hook—a #6 instead of a #8, and so on.

Force in Hook Setting

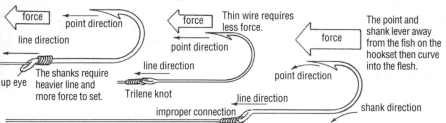

Up-eye hooks must be snelled to create direct pull, where line and hook point move in the same direction. On straight-eye hooks, tie directly with your favorite knot.

Hook Guide

Small (2- to 4-inch minnows) or leeches—#4 to 1/0 light-wire wide gap hooks (Eagle Claw 42, Daiichi D18, Gamakatsu 514 & 504)

Nightcrawlers—#8 to #2 baitholder hooks with barbs on the shank (Eagle Claw 181, Daiichi D24)

Medium (3- to 5-inch) minnows, crayfish, waterdogs and leopard frogs—#2 to 2/0 wide-gap hooks (Eagle Claw 42, Daiichi D18, Gamakatsu 514 & 504)

Large (6- to 10-inch) minnows (particularly shiners) and other large livebaits—1/0 to 10/0 wide-gap or kahle-style hooks (Eagle Claw 42 or 141, Gamakatsu 514)

Various livebaits in heavy cover situations—#1 to 4/0 hooks with wire weedguards (Eagle Claw 249WA or 151WA, Mustad 3369)

To avoid gut-hooking fish—1/0 to 6/0 circle hooks (Eagle Claw L702, Gamakatsu Circle Octopus, Daiichi Bleeding Bait Circle).

Hooks & Heads for Soft Plastic Baits

New hooks are designed for particular plastic baits or are weighted to give a different look to standard presentations. Jigheads also alter the action of worms, craws, tubes, grubs, and lizards. Lindy-Little Joe's Floatin' Fuzz-E-Grub is a floating, swimming jighead that raises Carolina-rigged baits higher off the bottom.

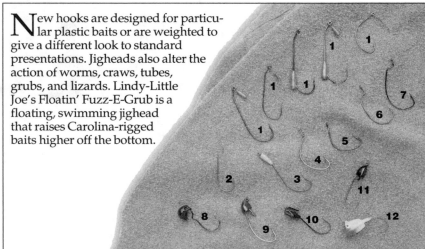

(1) Mustad Needle Power Lock Series; (2) 1/0 Tournament Lures Point Plus Shadoss; (3) 1/8 ounce hBlue Fox Hidden Head; (4) 3/0 Oldham's Mega-Bite; (5) 1/0 HP Hook; (6) 3/0 Owner Rig'N Hook; (7) 3/0 Gamakatsu EWG; (8) Bait Rigs Odd'ball Jig; (9) Legacy-Loc Jig; (10) Jaker; (11) Katsuichi Violence Jighead; (12) Lindy–Little Joe Floatin' Fuzz-E-Grub.

Circle Designs

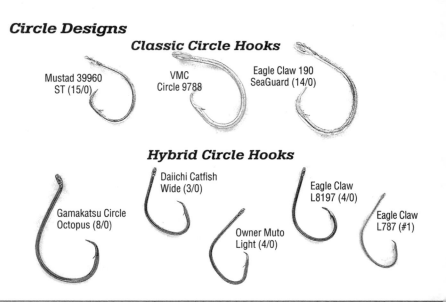

Classic Circle Hooks

Mustad 39960 ST (15/0)

VMC Circle 9788

Eagle Claw 190 SeaGuard (14/0)

Hybrid Circle Hooks

Gamakatsu Circle Octopus (8/0)

Daiichi Catfish Wide (3/0)

Owner Muto Light (4/0)

Eagle Claw L8197 (4/0)

Eagle Claw L787 (#1)

Components

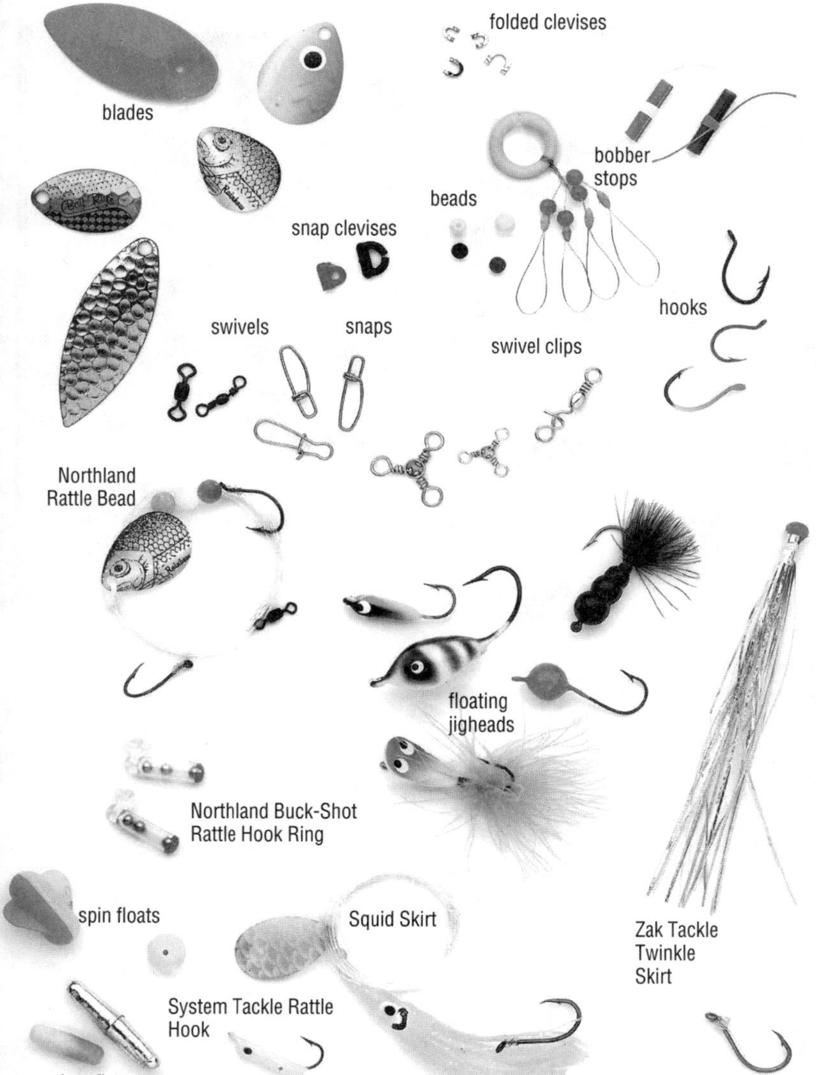

blades

folded clevises

bobber stops

snap clevises

beads

swivels

snaps

swivel clips

hooks

Northland Rattle Bead

floating jigheads

Northland Buck-Shot Rattle Hook Ring

spin floats

Squid Skirt

Zak Tackle Twinkle Skirt

System Tackle Rattle Hook

cigar floats

Sinker Types

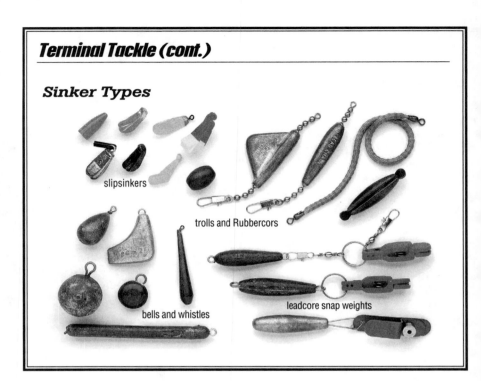

slipsinkers

trolls and Rubbercors

bells and whistles

leadcore snap weights